VINCE KARALIUS
A Rugby League Legend

MAURICE BAMFORD

VERTICAL EDITIONS

First published in the United Kingdom in 2006 by Vertical Editions, 7 Bell Busk, Skipton, North Yorkshire BD23 4DT

ISBN
1-904091-16-4
978-1-904091-16-5

Cover design and typeset by HBA, York

Printed and bound by the Cromwell Press, Trowbridge

CONTENTS

ACKNOWLEDGEMENTS

I must start by thanking Vince Karalius for allowing me to attempt to put into words the details of his fascinating and outstanding life. A whole book could have been written about his family or his business life or a myriad of other facets of this legend of my sport – Rugby League Football – and that is what constitutes my effort, the game he played.

I must admit that my first phone call to the Isle of Man to Vince and his wife Barbara, was, to me, like phoning the Pope. I must thank Vince's cousin, Tony Karalius, with whom I worked as coach of Wigan RLFC in the early 1980s. Tony was the one who gave me Vince's number and gave me the confidence to call the great man. Vince was everything Tony said he would be, a gentleman.

But just to tell stories of how great a player and coach Vince was would be insufficient. His standing in the game, to this day, can be judged by the people I must thank for their help in completing this work. The respected former rugby league writer for the *Yorkshire Post* and rugby league historian, Raymond Fletcher, who was kind enough to offer the foreword; Ray French, Wilf Smith, Alex Murphy, Austin Rhodes, Brian McGinn, George Parsons, Jim Mills and Neil Fox, each one a star within the game and each one has paid tribute to Vince in this book. Robert Gate helped me considerably as did Dr Tony Collins, both men being renowned and very well respected historians of the greatest game. The St Helens historians, Alex Service and Denis

Whittle, and Michael Flynn of the Widnes club too put me right with pictures and other aspects of Vince's career and I thank them all sincerely.

I would like to thank my wife Rita, who helped with the spelling. The times I called to her, 'Rita, how do you spell …?' must have been in the thousands. And finally my dad, the late Danny Bamford, for introducing me to the sweetest game of all, because if he hadn't I couldn't have written about Vince Karalius.

Maurice Bamford
January 2006

INTRODUCTION

What can one say about a legend? How can one possibly write about a man amongst men, who, in an era of outstandingly skilful and tough players, stood out like a beacon, like the Empire State building or the Eiffel Tower. Words are indeed inadequate to describe the emotions a spectator went through whilst watching this ultra fit athlete tear the guts out the opposition by the sheer ferocity of the most uncompromising tackling ever witnessed. Then, when carrying the ball, this athlete would release pin-point accurate passes to his supporting teammates or pull out of tackles and make clean breaks then send the man backing up away for a try. Yes, you either loved this man or you hated the sight of him because of the damage he did to your team. This man is Vincent Peter Patrick Karalius, Vince Karalius star player with St Helens, Widnes, Lancashire, England and Great Britain.

One of eight children with seven brothers and one sister, his grandparents hailed from Lithuania but his father was a Scotsman and his mum was from the Emerald Isle, Ireland. The number of the then family home in Hood Road, Widnes, Lancashire, held a strange, almost mystic future for the young Karalius as it was number 13!

A yardstick of a player's popularity is the number of bread and butter, ordinary Joe Spectator's who claim to be mates of the player and who 'know' all about what's going on with him.

We have all heard them, 'Oh yes, I was with so and so last week and he told me what went on in the game last weekend'. Well Vince Karalius must be in the Guinness Book of Records with the number of blokes who say to this day, 'Yes, Vince was a good pal of mine for years'. That was the strength of the man's personality and the absolute length of his popularity, both then, as a player and now as a long retired participant of the game as both player and coach. The respect generated by Vince Karalius was, and is, phenomenal. When elderly ex-players, who tested themselves as younger men against him, are asked, 'What was it like in those days to play in key matches against Karalius?' they will grimace and say, 'He was a hard bugger!' Then, wistfully, with a wry smile will add, 'but he was just about the best in the business when there were a lot of great loose forwards about!'

Vince's regular opponents read like a who's who of rugby league greats. As a nineteen year-old, twelve and a half stone loose forward, Vince came face to face with the then big hitters of professional rugby league, the Gee and Egan's of Wigan, Markham and Scott's of Hull, Wilkinson and Fearnley's of Halifax and the Tomlinson and Day's of Oldham. And in his autobiography, *Lucky Thirteen*, published back in 1964, Vince tells of his Saints debut in 1952 against a very tough Warrington outfit whose pack included the awesome duo of Jim Featherstone, of Great Britain fame and Australian international Harry Bath. The youngster had a very hard baptism indeed as every time he handled the ball, he '...seemed to be on the end of a mother and father of a good hiding'. But his best days playing rugby league were yet to come. As captain of the St Helens side and his successful tour of Australia and New Zealand in 1958, where he frightened the Aussies into submission, those were to be great days indeed.

The Widnes lad then finally arrived at the then home of the Widnes club, Naughton Park. He again achieved wonderful success on the pitch before entering into the 'thin ice' world of coaching. And once more Vince achieved the ultimate success on the other side of the touchline, coaching his home town club to two Wembley wins.

After retiring from rugby league, Vince was in demand for commentating on games on the radio and TV. Then following a long and successful business career, Vince retired to that jewel of the Irish Sea, the Isle of Man. But it was those halcyon days that began with a tough debut and encompassed winning visits to Wembley, Lancashire Cup successes, Championship Trophy wins and an Ashes winning tour, that cemented Vincent Peter Patrick Karalius in the British Rugby League's Hall of Fame, the St Helens club Hall of Fame and took the great man into the hearts of rugby league fans who witnessed his all out, perpetual motion, never defeated attitude. Let's hope that this book will help maintain Vince's true place in the traditions of our great game, that of the number one, number thirteen.

1

THE FAMILY, HOME AND ST MICHAEL'S IN DITTON

The local Roman Catholic school in Ditton, near Widnes had as Headmaster, a man of the old school. Eddie Murphy was his name and amongst his young charges were a family with an unusual family tree. One might say for the 1930s, a very unusual genealogy, for the youngsters of the family Karalius could boast grandparents from Lithuania and Tipperary in Ireland. To top that, the father of the youngsters, Brendan Karalius was a Scotsman, and his wife, Katy, the mother of the family, was a fair colleen from the Emerald Isle.

A staunch Catholic background gave the young Karalius clan a strong family bond and a typical tough, but fair, disciplined upbringing. Times were hard for a big family in the 1930s and not many families came bigger than Brendan and Katy's. With seven sons: Terence, Vincent, Lawrence, Dennis, Tony, Brendan and Frank, and in between Dennis and Tony, there was Eileen. Yes, eight kids. Four of the brothers went on to play professional rugby league: Terence, Dennis, Tony and Vincent of which two advanced onto the international scene with Tony representing Great Britain five times and Vincent playing in the revered Red, White and Blue jersey on twelve occasions.

If any man epitomises a period of greatness in our games history it is Vince Karalius. He was the foremost forward in an era of outstanding forwards, but more of that later, as this chapter is about the young Vince and his siblings and his mum and dad. I suppose a full book could be devoted to telling of the life and times of seven brothers and a sister in those tough times living through the end of the dreadful depression of the early 30s and an even more dreadful world war period in the early to middle 1940s.

Vince was born on 15 October 1932 in a house in Cameron Road. As the second oldest, Vince recalls that he and his brothers never knew how the family grew – Mum would be buzzing around the house, in would come a lady with a bag, Mum and the lady would go upstairs and a short time later, down would come another little brother! Soon the family moved into a four bedroom council house in Hood Road and a decent kicker of a ball could have punted from the house into Naughton Park, the home of Widnes RLFC. But it was the days under the guidance of Mr Eddie Murphy that Vince remembers with affection and he tells of Mr Murphy not only being a devout Catholic, but also a staunch loyalist. Now there's a thing! Every day at school leaving time, Mr Murphy would bang on his elevated desk with his headmaster's stick and say, 'Now children we will sing Rose of England', then with his Catholic hat on he would demand a highly emotive rendition of 'Faith of our Fathers'! Vince said that those kids left that school every afternoon and would have beaten Australia in a Test series they were so fired up. This was Vince's first lesson in motivation.

The Karalius boys were keen on sport and developed into very capable athletes. Vince's elder brother, the late Terence, was a superb all-rounder, playing rugby league for Liverpool Stanley and was a very good local cricketer – a fast bowler. Terence was known to break a stump in two, so quick were his deliveries. Dennis was a tough no-nonsense forward and was on both St Helens' and Warrington's books in his career. Tony, an excellent hooker in the days of competitive scrimmaging, was an international in his own right and his dummy half play was of the highest order. Tony had spells at Widnes, St Helens, Wigan and Fulham.

Eileen played a big part in the boys' lives as the only female apart from mother Katy in their close family. Lawrence and Frank were Vince's biggest fans and Brendan, although contracting polio when only a youngster continued the family's sports successes by becoming a very good swimmer. The great man smiles when he talks about the days of his childhood and the discipline that had to be maintained with such a big family. 'If my dad missed you, my mum caught you with one and it was hard to say which one could clout the hardest.'

Vince almost 'missed the boat' as a rugby league player as his first choice sport as a kid was indeed soccer. This big, rangy kid was a pretty good junior goalkeeper and fancied himself playing for Manchester City or United after beginning at school and progressing through to several junior soccer teams including the impressive-sounding Widnes ICI, and, in his early teens, Vince had aspirations of becoming another Frank Swift or Bert Trautman. But after being introduced to the thirteen-a-side game by watching local team Widnes with his brothers, he became captivated by the sport.

Then at 16, Vince signed to play junior rugby league football with that famous breeding ground of young players, West Bank ARLFC, and by doing so met a man who would help start a love affair with the game. The man was Frank Grayson, his team boss at West Bank and a real sergeant major character but a great bloke, whose rigid discipline and forthright manner endeared Vince to him. Coach Grayson obviously saw a winner in the young Karalius and spent time on a one-on-one basis with Vince. Being an astute coach and a very shrewd tactician, Frank worked on Vince's youthful flaws and even advised him over which position to play that best suited him – number 13.

Vince still insists that a few sessions with Frank Grayson as coach would sort out the wheat from the chaff from any team and his theme on discipline didn't end with game tactics; it continued into how to physically turn out for matches. Frank would hold a boot inspection before every game and inspect the soles of the boots, studs and even laces. His instructions were to clean and polish sides, tops, toes and soles of your boots until they shone and laces had to be washed to their natural white colour. This had to be done when you arrived home after playing mostly on rutted pitches, in slime, mud, rain and snow then changing in all sorts of huts, barns, old sheds and tin shelters. The only thing that was consistent was that the container and liquid you washed away the caked mud with after the match was a bucket of cold water! And that had to do for the whole team.

Like most junior rugby league players of that era this was the welcome that greeted them when they took the plunge into the tough, no-nonsense world of the greatest game and it all served to weld Vince's enthusiasm to the handling code, the rough and tumble, the no moans from players who took a hard knock, the team spirit and the sheer comradeship that playing this hardest of competitive sports fosters. Vince recalls how this friendship and trust in each other evolved as the team developed into a belief of near invincibility, the 'We can't lose' feeling.

Indeed, the side at West Bank had a far better team spirit than some of the highly paid professional teams in the Lancashire area and this spirit was kindled in no small way because of the hours and hours of togetherness of playing touch rugby, which hones the awareness skills so necessary in the main game of rugby league. Vince insists that touch rugby was played on every piece of spare ground in the towns of south-west Lancashire, as it certainly was in the towns of the West Riding of Yorkshire in those days. This team spirit at West Bank was one of the reasons why Vince's team did so well and always in the background was the common sense lead from the father figure, Frank Grayson.

But boys will be boys and I shudder to think what Frank Grayson's blood pressure would have been had he known the antics that Vince and his mate, Alan Winstanley, were up to one summer evening when both youngsters were about sixteen years old. Now young Karalius was a daredevil, scared of very little and his buddy young Winstanley was just as bad. The idea dawned on both the tough, young West Bank players that they would dive off the Runcorn Bridge into the River Mersey, swim the short distance to Oglet then run home. There was another conspirator to this deed, one Gordon Carney, who was a slightly smaller player than both Vince and Alan and was not allowed to dive with them, but nonetheless was given a very important job to do. He was instructed to carry the clothes of both divers to a place near to Vince's house so they could dress there and go home without causing a fuss. The daring divers, on seeing the awesome distance twixt lip of bridge handrail and top of Mersey, suddenly developed 'cold feet' and decided, at the eleventh hour, to change the venue and jump, not dive, off the old railway bridge into the Manchester Ship Canal, as full knowledge of the depth of water was not known! No one can remember if either jumper called out 'Geronimo' as the fearless pair stepped out into air, but step they did, and if it had happened today the pair would have been sponsored to the hilt and made the West Bank club a fair bit richer.

Nowadays I suppose the two boys would be classed as hooligans, but I guess the thinking these days is more towards safety and that it is the rescuers who are put at risk. Back then the actions were called 'high spirits' and only now, years later, when we are old enough to realise the dreadful dangers that both Vince and Alan faced, would we wince at the chances they took. But I guess it typifies Vince and his pal as neither of these two hard lads would want to lose face in front of each other as they both held tremendous respect for each others strength of character and willpower.

Vince still speaks in glowing terms of Alan Winstanley, and his courage but, like so many good young teenage rugby league prospects, Alan failed to make the full transition from the junior amateur league into the then ultra competitive professional game, sadly because tough as he was, he did not grow from being a big lad into a big man and this factor was a major one in those days.

Anyway the dynamic duo hit the water of the Manchester Ship Canal and not only swam to safety but also into Widnes folklore for if Vincent Karalius had not made it in rugby league, he at least would always be remembered for his courage, with Alan Winstanley, in that exhilarating plunge into the Ship Canal.

Vince had left the security of St Michaels Roman Catholic School a few weeks short of his fourteenth birthday to make his way in the world. He had a job though before he left school, that of delivery boy for Mrs Mercer who owned a corner shop grocers near to Vince's home. His transport for the deliveries was a huge bicycle with a big iron basket on the front, the old butcher's bike! Not long in the job, Mrs Mercer asked Vince to deliver an order to a lady not far from the shop and amongst the butter and eggs was a piece of Mrs Mercer's home made slab cake, a mouth-watering confection holding various super fruits, currents and raisins. Everyone ordered a piece of Mrs Mercer's slab cake, either for special events or as a weekend treat.

The order was for one half pound of slab cake and on weighing it out; Mrs Mercer found it to be just short of the required measure and topped it up with a thin slice of slab cake. Now if the total cake arrived at its destination we will never know, but our intrepid young delivery boy was known to be particularly partial to slab cake!

Vince's first job on leaving school was to work for the huge ICI company and like a lot of good Catholic lads in those days, Vince gave his first week's wage to the church. Enrolling at night school Vince was determined to do well and sat and passed his exams and at the conclusion of his apprenticeship became a qualified boilermaker. It was in the ICI sports section that Vince continued his school sport of soccer and started making a name for himself as a promising goalkeeper.

However, like most kids in Widnes, Vince had played touch and pass and stood on the terraces at Naughton Park supporting his home town club, the 'Chemics' and he had lived near to the famous old ground all of his life. His dad, Brendan, although born in Scotland, had been brought up in the area of West Bank, down by the river, where his Lithuanian born parents had a bakehouse, and West Bank was a rugby league area. So Brendan suggested to Vince that he might consider having a run-out with West Bank, who had a tremendous reputation of being one of the best sides in the Widnes and St Helens district. And from there began the rugby league journey that led to the legend of Vincent Peter Patrick Karalius, Vince Karalius of Saints, Widnes, Lancashire, England and Great Britain.

In those days to play junior rugby league a lad had to have a

fair amount of courage and determination. The organised
BARLA leagues of today bear little comparison to those
austere days when players performed their skills in the most
spartan of conditions. Yet those same conditions, so
unacceptable today, produced a veritable wealth of great
professional players and top class amateurs. Youth clubs,
Working Men's clubs, Amateur rugby league clubs and
almost every district turned out teams from around under 16
years of age upwards. And very strong leagues operated in
most West Riding and North-West towns. West Bank was
one of those teams in one of those strong leagues. In Vince's
time at the club, the teams he played in – Under-16s to
Under-18s – were regular winners of local cups and
championships.

West Bank's biggest rivals were United Services of St
Helens and St Patricks of Widnes. But about the time Vince
went to West Bank, the Widnes professional club embarked
on a youth policy in which they embraced all the good young
players from the local schools and formed a new team,
Naughton Park Rangers, from whom, it was hoped, would
emerge the future backbone of the Widnes club. The lads
from West Bank rose to the new challenge and managed to
hold on to the unofficial title of 'best junior side in Widnes'
by defeating the Rangers by a convincing score.

Through Vince's two years at West Bank, under the
watchful eye of his junior coach and mentor, Frank Grayson,
his development as a tough-tackling and skilful ball-playing
loose forward didn't go unnoticed. Peter Lyons had moved,
as trainer, from Naughton Park, Widnes, to Knowsley Road,
St Helens, and Peter had seen this blockbusting, teak-tough
youngster playing at West Park and liked what he saw. Vince
had talks with Peter Lyons and the new trainer convinced
this eighteen year-old prospect to 'have a go at Saints' for six

trial games. In *Lucky Thirteen*, Vince tells of Saints wanting to sign him after two trial games but the shrewd youngster wanted to be certain that all was well with his game in the professional league and opted to play all the six games. Those extra four games that Vince wanted to play only strengthened the Saints' directors faith in signing him and so he put pen to paper for a one-off signing fee of £200, which was about the norm that professional clubs paid to juniors in those days.

The law only gave a player one bite at the money then as any other payment either by his club or any other club was illegal. The payment was classed as an inducement for the player to surrender his amateur status. The only other payment from the player's club was a benefit payment granted after ten seasons' unbroken service, or very infrequently, a payment by an insurance company if a player had to end his career because of injury. But this law was broken almost every time a player changed clubs with what became known as a 'back-hander' or 'sweetener'. This was an agreed amount of money, always in cash, that the player received for signing with his new club. A couple of smarter clubs would keep their books spotlessly clean by paying the selling club a little above the asking price for the player and let the selling club pay the back-hander to their departing player, thus the buying club remained whiter than white.

So the plucky lad who served as an altar boy, delivered the slab cake, jumped off the railway bridge into the Ship Canal and was learning to be a boilermaker, was now a professional rugby league player and was the world at his feet? Not quite yet, that was a few short seasons away!

2

SAINTS, BREAKING THE ICE, AND THE ARMY

At eighteen years old and coming straight out of junior rugby football the next stage of any youngster's education was a spell in the A team (or reserves in soccer parlance). Now some people, for years, condemned the A teams as a waste of time and money, as they considered it to be a home for no-hopers and players who would never make the grade. Well, I suppose there could be an argument for that, but the A teams were, in my opinion, a tremendous vehicle for blooding young talent, as a fitness vehicle for returning players after injury and the vital means for looking at trialists from both codes of Rugby Football.

In the days when Vince signed for Saints, there were two separate A team leagues, the Yorkshire Senior Competition and the Lancashire Combination. Both leagues had their own Challenge Cups and Championship Trophies, and many fine players, and indeed international players, came through the old system. This was the world of rugby league that Vince found himself in 1950. Good players, at the back end of their careers, a few down and out nutters who played only for the kudos of fighting as many times as they could over the eighty minutes of a game, a few played for beer money but the majority were youngsters feeling their way and learning from the old heads who took the time to put the kids right and hopefully then kick on to better things within the game.

One big bonus for Vince was that at St Helens he was again under the watchful eye of a great man and great coach. Just as at West Bank, when he first arrived and met Frank Grayson, this time Vince was enthralled by the great Jim Sullivan. It was very much a learning time for Vince when he began his career at the excellent Saints club in that winter of 1951. It didn't take the youngster long to realise just what was needed to reach the top in this he-man game of professional Rugby League. But Vince was fortunate in that he had both the mental and, with much hard training, the physical attributes that were required to make the grade.

Talking to senior players and always listening to his coach, that was Frank Grayson's input, Vince was reminded regularly that rugby league forwards never, never took a backward step. Even on the end of a good hiding, if at all possible, one stood one's ground and attempted to give, at least, as much as you got. Strength, fitness and more strength and fitness took a player a third of the way there. Bravery was another third and skills were the final third. Of course the golden touch was natural pace and balance and if a player was fortunate enough to have that lot he was usually 'made'.

Another facet required was sometimes beyond a player's ability to do well, this facet was luck. Now there used to be a saying amongst professional players that, 'You make your own luck'. I tend to disagree as sometimes a player has no control over serious injury, some unfortunately pick up injuries that finish them as a player, some show real character by making a comeback after serious injury, but alas some can't do that as the injury may well be too serious. That's rank bad luck. If your career is a long one and you manage to escape serious injury, then that is lucky and fair play to you.

Every player who made the grade at international level had, at some time in his career, a slice of luck. It could be that he was in the right place at the right time, or that he was naturally big, strong and fit, or, he met up with a Frank Grayson or Jim Sullivan!

Vince quickly learned the importance, to the supporters of St Helens, of winning matches, particularly the crunch derby matches against local rivals Wigan, in league, cup, home or away! But in this environment he had a big asset, he was a natural winner and second prizes were of no use to him. To Vince, the winning of games therefore gaining winning money for doing so, was everything. In today's financial climate of Super League, the player is full time and, usually, on a lucrative contract. Football is his job, and the cream on the cake is that extra appearance fee – win or lose! Whereas, in the 1950s a player held down a day job, he was a policeman, a teacher, a boilermaker or whatever, and trained on Tuesday and Thursday evenings after work at his club. The match winning money supplemented the meagre earnings of those days and recompensed the time and effort spent training and playing after a hard weeks work.

A number of the top clubs trained an extra evening, but even so, one thing that was insisted on by all coaches, was that the player 'did a bit away from the club, on his own'. Now this training could have been with weights at home or in a local gym, extra road work, running, to build up one's stamina or working in a park with grass under foot and gaining invaluable strength and speed with both long and short sprints.

These were things Vince did in a clever and determined strength and fitness programme to make himself bigger, fitter and stronger than the opposition. There were some bigger men than Vince in his day, but not many as fit or as strong as he was. His handling skills were honed on hours of passing and catching a rugby ball and, with the help of younger brother Dennis, he gradually developed the skill that he realised was so necessary to improve his game, rhythm. To quote Vince from *Lucky Thirteen*, 'I spent hours just passing the ball to Dennis and taking his return pass in our back yard at home. Pass, pass, pass, simply flicking the ball to one another to learn the rhythm of passing and handling, to pick up the speed of delivery and accuracy in taking and giving a pass'. Vince also built up his fitness by acting on the advice of his coach and undertaking a ten mile training session where he intermixed walking with 200 yard sprints. He also did a little something which is unique in rugby league training: Vince's mum had a full-length dressing mirror in her wardrobe and he would spend time in front of that mirror just gently tossing the ball from hand to hand, watching his own movements as he swayed to the rhythm of hand and eye co-ordination. Vince explains, 'It's like dancing. If you have rhythm you can dance, once you have acquired the correct rhythm in football it should never leave you.'

Vince's philosophy on fitness and skills practices were well before his time. Even in his early days as a young professional he was thinking all the time how he could break into the world of the top players. His natural winning mindset gradually came to the fore too. He was one of the first English players to practice individual pre-match preparation. One reads that the American sports psychiatrists, who earn their livelihoods in the various professional grid-iron football, basketball, ice hockey and baseball leagues, came up with this idea. You imagine yourself in a game situation, say making a tackle. In your mind, you make the tackle, a great tackle, a match-winning tackle, or you see yourself intercept a pass and run the length of the field, beating man after man. The thoughts are always positive, always a winner. This is how Vince Karalius prepared for matches before the kick-off. His winning mindset prepared him to make those all-devouring tackles, slip out those deft passes and target a dangerous opponent before he set foot on the field. Mental preparation, as preached by the sports psychiatrist. Well Vince was doing this very thing before the Americans invented it!

After Vince signed for the Saints on 16 August 1951 he spent almost all that first season taking his first steps on the professional rugby league learning curve in the A team. Amongst his teammates also in the A team was Walter Delves, a second row forward who was signed four months after Vince from the enemies of his amateur days at West Bank, the very good United Services juniors. The Saints pack in the A team must have taken some shifting with the young Delves and Karalius in it, as both were tough, no-nonsense, hard-tackling lads. The local weekly newspaper gradually began to mention Vince in its A team match reports and in one victory over Whitehaven, up at the old Recreation Ground, it was noted that, 'The St. Helens forwards, with the back three outstanding, played very well and paved the way for the three-quarters to score the tries, Delves, Karalius and King playing excellent football'.

Now anyone who can remember the legendary Vince Karalius playing may well have a little smile when Vince states seriously that he was not a dirty player. Indeed he admits to playing the game to the limit of the laws and playing it as hard and as tough as he could. Nothing wrong with that, it is what the ordinary Joe Spectator wants to see for his money. Vince detested low-down fouls. But to remind the reader of how the game was in those days and of how much it meant to gain winning money, plus the dark humour that surrounded these incidents, I must return to Walter Delves. Vince and Walter were playing together in one game when Walter was involved in a fracas with an opponent who had to be assisted from the field. This was of course in the days before substitutes and it left the opposing team badly up against it being a man short. The incident didn't sit right with Vince and he pulled Walter during a short stoppage in the game to remonstrate with the tough forward. After listening to Vince's complaints Walter's cool reply was, 'Right or wrong Vince, there are only twelve of the buggers now'.

Towards the end of Vince's first season and after a series of good reports of form from the A team, his big chance came in the first team when, on Wednesday, 2 April 1952, he was selected to play at loose forward in the away fixture against Warrington. So at nineteen years old, with limited A team experience and weighing in at only 12st 10lb, the youngster was thrown against a fearsome pack that included the Great Britain front rower, Jim Featherstone, the experienced hooker Ike Fishwick and the rugged Australian legend, Harry Bath. And the man Vince would have to overcome at number seven was the brilliant international scrum-half, Gerry Helme who had the powerful Ally Naughton in his centres with the King of the wingmen, the fabulous Brian Bevan, on one flank. The Saints pack included Australian Max Garbler and the tough Bill Bretherton in the second row and young Vince, at number 13.

The result of the game was a good win for St Helens by 13 points to 5 and a healthy 13,000 crowd saw the side work hard for their victory. Now from this debut by Vince comes a tale that has been handed down through the years and Vince told himself that 'Next time you Warrington forwards will meet a different Vince Karalius'. Despite playing really well and gaining the desired winning money as well as a very good write-up in the newspaper, Vince took the mother and father of a good hiding from the bigger, older, far more experienced Warrington forwards, one Harry Bath in particular. The catalogue of stick he took on his debut included stiff arm tackles, round house right-handers, hooks and the knee into the stomach, and these were just some of the unexpected fouls. But it made Vince realise that to match these juggernauts in the future and to be able to gain retribution, he would have to be bigger and stronger. Wilf Smith, who played many times at half-back for Saints with Vince, recalls that, even though he signed four years after the young Karalius, the tale of Vince's debut was still talked of. The battered youngster vowed and declared that such treatment would never again happen to him and it seemed to fire up something in Vince that would make him an even harder and tougher competitor. He himself calls it a hate complex. This hate was to become as much a part of his game as his passing or his tackling. The hatred was not aimed solely at the Warrington pack of forwards but towards all the other bigger, more experienced forwards who might fancy taking liberties with him. The hatred was in fact a grudge against almost every man who stood before Vince in those eighty minutes of football each week. To become bigger and stronger than he already was almost turned Vince into a hermit. As he says in *Lucky Thirteen* all he did was train, train, train. Weights, exercises, more weights, until he bulked up and hardened up.

Having little time to recover after his debut, Vince was

included in the team to play Hull FC at the Boulevard three days after his first outing against Warrington. It was Saturday, 5 April 1952 when Vince made his second appearance for Saints. Now without a doubt one of the toughest teams to play at that time was Hull. Only a few short seasons later the giant East Riding pack would contest the major trophies and Vince's second game was nonetheless a tough one.

The big men in Hull's forwards were Des Foreman, Bob Coverdale, the 6ft 4in dock policeman Harry Markham, and Arthur Bedford. Colin Hutton the former Widnes full-back was at number 13 and Aussie Keith Gittoes and Ivor Watts were the flying wingmen. The centres were the player-coach, Roy Francis and a young John Whiteley. Don Burnell was at number 7 and his partner at stand-off was the strong running Conway.

Despite another good game by Vince the result was a defeat for Saints by 14 points to 7, so our hero had tasted victory and defeat in three days. Vince admits that he felt as though he had been hit by a steam roller as the hammering by the Warrington pack, added to eighty minutes against the Airlie Birds at the Boulevard took its toll on the youngster. In this match, Vince looked after his Saints scrum-half, Tommy Finn, who in fact moved across to the Boulevard and played against Wigan for Hull in the 1959 Wembley Challenge Cup final.

Part of Vince's pre-match preparation was to arrive at the ground as late as possible so that he was not sat around in the dressing room waiting for the kick-off. This was his thing, his way and it worked for him. Some players like to arrive early and have a laugh and joke with their teammates, others have their own pre-match rituals, a walk around the ground to see the condition of the pitch, stop to talk with the early arrived spectators. Then came the dressing-room rituals. Some did their own strapping, applying tapes and bandages to old injuries, the effect being more psychological than medical, thumbs taped, fingers taped and webbed to stop breaking or splitting, knee bandages, figure of eight shoulder strapping, shoulder pads, hookers with their shins protected by layers of pads and wadding, anything to absorb the kicks and stampings they were sure to receive, and finally, the bottle that was in most dressing rooms, Ammonium Carbonate, which chemists called Sal Volatile, but we in Yorkshire called 'Salvolatally'. This genuine concoction was said to settle your stomach, but in a lot of cases only made one feel bloody awful. Some clubs had a bottle of sherry in the dressing room before a game as one of its qualities was said to have a calming effect on the drinker! But as stated, Vince's thing was to prepare his hate complex and not be disturbed by the goings-on around him in the dressing room, hence, arrive as late as possible, strip and out and at 'em! Possibly the term 'hate complex' may seem strange when used in the context of a sporting game. Vince uses another term also about his approach to his professional sport which is, 'killer instinct'. This is at its zenith only in the eighty minutes of a game and does not imply that Vince would deliberately break the laws of the game through foul play but he did play the game in a tremendously hard way with no quarter asked nor given and, he played it hard, up to the very edge of the laws of the game.

At the close of his first season, Vince was still only nineteen. He had the Warrington and Hull games under his belt when Saints three-match end-of-season tour of France arrived. The young loose forward was told that he was included in the club's touring squad so he packed his case and off to Toulouse he went with his teammates. The itinerary of the short tour read thus, Toulouse, Tarascon-sur-Ariège and Figeac. The French authorities pulled a flanker on the St Helens club by not mentioning that the Toulouse side would indeed be the full French national side who were to play England shortly. So it was Saints v France in Toulouse!

Because it was the end of the season, the Knowsley Road squad had several first-team players missing because of injuries and various other commitments. The regulars who did play were Dougie Greenall, 'Todder' Dickinson, George Langfield, Alan Prescott, Bill Whittaker, Bill Bretherton, George Parsons and Vince Karalius. The young Vince scored a try and Langfield kicked a goal in the unsurprising defeat by 35 points to 5. George Langfield was the former Castleford scrum half who left Saints and went, as did Tommy Finn, to Hull FC.

After that opening match, the senior members of the Saints squad all agreed that the French had improved out of all proportion and were sure that they would give the England side a good run for their money.

In the second game at Tarascon, the Saints team was unrecognisable – positionally at least. The three-quarter line was made up of four forwards – Cheetham, Stott, Karalius and Prescott – all big men! Now Alan Prescott, who went on to earn everlasting fame as the Great Britain captain who played on with a broken arm to lead his men to victory against the Australians in 1958, had indeed experience on the wing as he played there as a young Halifax player. But against the vastly improving French, the patched up Saints had no chance and went down by 45 points to 5, Langfield kicking their goal and Prescott, turning the clock back, with a typical powerful try. The young, fast, skilful French backs gave their visitors the old fashioned run-round and the Saints had no answer for it.

In the final game at Figeac, Vince was rested and against all the odds, his mates managed a cracking win by 27 points to 24 against a team that included established internationals and a smattering of players considered to be future internationals. This memorable win was spearheaded by Bill Whittaker, who had a storming game and figured amongst the try scorers.

So on to early September 1952: the French experience behind Vince and with one foot in the door of the St Helens first team. The Saints' season had just started and the 1952 Australian touring side had arrived in the UK, with all the Aussie media saying that under the captaincy of the fabulous Clive Churchill, they stood a great chance of returning to Oz with the Ashes. Churchill, South Sydney's superb full-back, known in Australia as the 'Little Master', because of his diminutive size but tremendous playing ability, headed a big, strong team that bulged with talent. Players of the calibre of Brian Carlson, Noel Pidding, Harry Wells, Tommy Ryan, Noel Hazzard, Denis Flannery, Des McGovern, Keith Holman and Greg Hawick were expected to achieve the ultimate objective, which was to win the Test series and these speed merchants were fronted by an enormous pack of forwards which included, Duncan Hall, Charlie Gill, Roy Bull, Brian Davies, Arthur Collinson, Tom Tyrell, Ken Kearney, Kevin Schubert, Harold Crocker and Col Donohoe.

As the fixture against the Aussie tourists approached, the Saints team attracted a couple of injuries in the ongoing early league programme and the very good Saints side would be without five regular first team players for this all-star clash against the Australian side. The game was played on 27 September 1952 and the Saints team, short of the five regulars, was: Lowe; Dickinson, Greenall (Captain), Roach, McCormick; Honey, Langfield; Prescott, Blakemore, Parr, Thornett, Bretherton, Karalius. Vince quickly realised that his star was on the rise and that this was a great opportunity to push up another rung on the first team ladder. A good game would help his cause to reach for the top.

Most players can recall the game or incident that cemented their station in life or in their chosen sport. Sometimes they are called 'stepping stones in one's career'. This was the moment for him. Returning again to *Lucky Thirteen*, Vince tells how he felt in the build-up to his biggest game up to then. How he tried to talk himself into believing that they were only men, human beings and that this game was just another game, nothing special. He remembers how he retired to bed early, much earlier than normal, trying to ensure a good rest and a long night's sleep. But sleep would not come and even reading a thriller did not help. It suddenly dawned on him that he was suffering something new for him. It was big match nerves. He had never had this feeling before. Vince knew that he had to get some rest and also knew how vital it was to relax and sleep well before the headlong physical explosion of the coming battle with the Aussies. What could be done? Why, of course his rhythm practice. Out of bed he climbed and into his mum's empty bedroom carrying his old rugby ball that he and his brother Dennis had passed so many hundreds of times. Standing in front of mum's dressing mirror he remembered the routines of the rhythm, moving the ball from one hand to the other, swaying to the handling beat. His confidence returned quickly and a relaxed feeling came over him, he returned to his bed and soon fell into a level, restful sleep.

Now this was 27 September 1952 and Vince was born on 15 October 1932 making him eighteen days short of his 20th birthday. He was not playing on the wing, or even in the centre. This kid, not yet 20 years old, was playing in the forwards against one of the biggest, hardest packs in the game! And only four and a half short months ago he was on the end of a hiding from a lesser Warrington pack. Vince showed a determination and toughness unusual in one so young. The Australians came to St Helens with their 'tails up'. Played seven, won six, drawn one was their proud record. Saints were without five regular first choice players, the best their supporters could hope for would be a brave performance from their favourites, yet there was still a feeling that the Saints just might give the tourists their hardest club game of the tour, or so they wished! As far as the young Karalius was concerned he was cool. The nerves had passed the night before, no worries and the still teenage loose forward forced himself to produce his best game so far in the Saints colours.

History tells of a fantastic victory for the depleted Lancashire heroes by 26 points to 8 and match reports of the game pinpoint George Langfield, with a superb display of goal kicking in which he landed seven from eight attempts, as one of the stars along with his half-back partner, Jimmy Honey. Amongst the forwards, Alan Prescott, Bill Bretherton, George Parr and Vince Karalius shone. Another newspaper stated that, 'Karalius linked with and covered for his half backs with an efficiency which promises well for the future'.

Possibly this one excellent performance against the

touring Australians was just the final push that offered Vince the chance of greatness, and despite all his fantastic successes in this hardest of all team sports, he still fills with pride when he remembers that great result with a weakened Saints team that beat the fearsome 1952 Aussie tourists, who, lost only three games on that tour – and the other two were against Great Britain!

In June 1952, St Helens appointed the fabulous Jim Sullivan as the new coach. He was an icon of the game and had won and done everything as player, captain and coach. His CV was akin to reading a who's who of the game including three time tourist to Australia, captain in 1932, and winner of the Challenge Cup several times as both player and coach. Vince had joined the Saints in August 1951 and made his debut in April 1952, at the end of a mediocre season when they finished in the bottom half of the table. Jim Sullivan signed a five-year contract at Saints but made an immediate impression on the club and its players, especially Vince Karalius.

Vince identified Big Jim with his former junior coach, Frank Grayson. Not the same men by any means but very similar in many ways. Jim Sullivan was all things to all men at Knowsley Road. A strict disciplinarian, straight as a die, a father figure who would listen to your problem and come up with an answer, a superb thinking coach in attack and defence, a great reader of a game and a man who knew the strengths and weaknesses of the opponents.

Jim Sullivan saw in Vince the two major disciplines that make great players: bravery and a total dedication to fitness. Vince remembers his simple philosophy, 'Be happy with yourself, get your team happy, and you will have a town and supporters who are football happy'. That is what he did at

Saints and, within nine months, he had led last season's bottom half of the table side to Wembley in the 1953 Challenge Cup final. He had the same players with the only newcomer, the terrific full back signed from Salford, the Welshman, Glyn Moses. The league placings had changed too for Saints were top of the league and with a record never held before at Knowsley Road, in that they were undefeated in their first eighteen away games of that season. The Lancashire League Championship was theirs too and they were the runners-up in the Lancashire Cup, having lost to Leigh in the final at Station Road, Swinton, by 22 points to 5. So as the club looked to Wembley and their opponents, the very good Yorkshire outfit Huddersfield, in that 1953 final, to the Saints and young Karalius, still five months short of his 21st birthday, things were very good indeed.

Jim Sullivan made a massive impact on Vince. Other players too fell under the Welshman's spell as the clubs' players gradually accepted the utter brilliance of this man allied to his personality and knowledge of the game he now coached. But the Huddersfield camp too had a crafty Welshman in charge as their coach, one Bill Smith, who had won at Wembley before when in charge of the Leeds side in the 18 points to 2 win over Warrington in the 1936 final. Vince was disappointed in being only in the squad of sixteen players on Wembley duty but accepted that the more experienced Welshman from Pontypool, Ray Cale, was possibly the better choice on the day. Ray Cale was not the only Welshman on duty for Saints that day at the twin towers. Abertillery wingman Steve Llewellyn, Pontypool tough centre, Don Gullick, ex Newport hooker, Reg Blakemore, former Abertillery second rower long serving George Parsons and the brilliant Glyn Moses at full back were all true men from the Principality.

Huddersfield would only have been slight underdogs going into this big game as they were the only team to have avoided defeat by Saints at some time that season. In October 1952 the Fartowners beat Saints at Knowsley Road by 17 points to 14 before a crowd of 22,000 and on 6 April 1953, Saints went to Fartown and forced a draw, 10 apiece, seen by 30,818. The Cup final was played on 25 April 1953 and is known in rugby league folklore as 'Young Ramsden's Match'. Peter Ramsden was nineteen years old on the Cup Final day, he not only suffered a broken nose early on but also scored the winning try and played a blinder. His display won him the highly cherished Lance Todd Trophy – presented in the name of the famous New Zealand and Wigan player and Salford coach – for the best and fairest player of the Cup Final. A wonderful award! The gate at Wembley was 89,588. Saints lost this prestigious final by 15 points to 10.

The Saints players felt terrible as they collected their losers' medals, mainly as they considered they had let down the coach, Jim Sullivan. They did, however, feel a lot better seven days later when St Helens destroyed Huddersfield at home, in the top four play-off with a runaway victory by 46 points to nil, in front of 32,000 spectators and seven days later again, took on the tough, rugged Halifax side in the old Championship Final, played as it was in those days, at the Maine Road home of Manchester City FC when 51,083 spectators attended. Saints' true form surfaced and a win by 24 points to 14 gave the experienced Big Jim something to smile about. Not a bad season's work. The Championship Cup, Lancashire League winners and runners-up in the two other big cups: the Lancashire Cup and the Challenge Cup.

Vince and all the team were at a celebration end of season party when Duggie Greenall, the club skipper, presented the coach with a travelling case on behalf of the players, saying that all the squad were better players since he joined them from Wigan. 'Sully' replied that the club had made a fine start under his leadership and winning the two trophies had shown consistency, 'But lads, next season I'm looking forward to an even better record'. As Vince says, 'That was Sully, never really satisfied if there was a place on the mantelpiece for another trophy or two'. But Vince listened intently to Big Jim when the ace coach came out with his wonderful words of wisdom that dovetailed into his making a point, 'A quarter of an hour's hard work in a match is worth an hour running aimlessly about on the training ground if a player is putting all he has got into it'.

Although the main man was monitoring Vince's good progress, so too were the journalists. Banging the drum for him because of his classic handling and running with the ball style, the 'journos' were, almost to a man, urging the selection of young Vince into the regular loose forward slot. But the steady, softly, softly progress that eased Vince into stardom was down mainly to the great man-management skills of Jim Sullivan. Others helped to mould Vince with sound advice and help on the field and he is only too willing to praise the assistance given by slightly older teammates, Alan Prescott, Bill Bretherton, Duggie Greenall, Steve Llewellyn and Glyn Moses in this, his major learning period. But he was now nearing 21 years of age, it was the time not only to serve St Helens but to serve his country, by two years of National Service in the armed forces.

Vince, being a boilermaker-blacksmith, was called to the

Royal Engineers to perform his basic training prior to his first posting. His induction into the forces began an important period of his sporting life. Shortly after his basic training was completed it was noticed that this supremely fit and athletically built young man was also intelligent and enthusiastic enough to be able to instruct others in the art and craft of fitness. The army being the army whisked him across to Aldershot and put Vince through a course as a Physical Training Instructor, a PTI, which also carried an automatic promotion up to lance corporal. Fit as he was, Vince found himself in very good company as one of the chief instructors was Olympic athlete Nick Stewart.

The regimented life, the regular food and the continuous sporting environment plus his own determination to be bigger, faster and stronger than the next man, ensured Vince was in his element for the next eighteen months. One sports writer hit the nail on the head when he wrote 'Vince Karalius is a role model for any youngster wanting to bulk up. A boilermaker-blacksmith by trade, his call-up was deferred until he was 21 years old when he was around 12st 7lbs. Wanting to keep fit for his game of rugby league he found there was no football at his South of England posting so he went for every kind and type of sport he could get. Weight lifting, basketball, gymnastics, physical culture, anything that built up his physique and added more muscle. The PTI's had never seen such a positive attitude towards fitness and strength and they marvelled at this young professional rugby league player, who yet had to make his name in this tough sport, who was so dedicated and willing to work for what he wanted for himself. The end product is that young Karalius came out of the army weighing over fourteen stones and was superbly fit and strong.'

Vince had been posted, as a PTI, to Liss in Hampshire and apart from the usual courses and odd moves on orders, spent most of his National Service time there. At the Army School of Physical Training in Adershot, Vince had struck up a friendship with another sportsman who did well as a professional boxer. He was Phil Edwards who boxed as a middleweight and actually took on the British, Commonwealth and indeed World middleweight champion, Terry Downes, twice, but unfortunately lost on both occasions against the tough Londoner. Vince says that in the barracks he would jump on Edwards and playfully rough him up, rugby league style, saying to the battling Welshman, 'How can you win fights, you're not strong enough', then Edwards would settle into his boxing stance and Vince would crash him with one of his all-embracing tackles and both big lads would collapse laughing at each other. One wonders if Vince had realised Phil's potential as a middleweight in future years, would he have jumped on his back and crash tackled him? Well I think he would have, just for the crack. One experienced writer once wrote of Vince that '…if he could have fought Mohammed Ali in a phone box, then Vince would have been the next heavyweight champion of the World!'

At the end of his National Service in November 1955, Vince left the army as the almost perfect fighting machine and one of the most dangerous and fearless forwards of his era. Vince had only managed to get a few weekends off, on leave, in the winter of the 1954-55 season and, whenever possible, had come back up north to play for Saints, wanting to prove himself as a first team squad member. But the Army needed him too and as the rugby league season started in August, Vince's two jobs clashed. Because of his sporting prowess and his superb fitness, Vince was a regular in the PTI's regimental team, representing them in the 440 yards sprint and the shot put and was irreplaceable. Now the sergeant-major who was in charge at Liss was a regular soldier and a Welshman. He was Sergeant-Major Knight, and a stickler for discipline. Just before Vince signed off duty on Friday lunchtime the fearsome NCO called Vince to him. 'Now listen Karalius, you know that the regimental sports day is on Monday and you know how important it is for us to do well. You are our key man in the 440 and the shot so I say to you, do not be late back on Monday morning as I want no slip ups.' Vince was determined not to let anyone down and vowed that he would be back at Liss in good time the following Monday morning.

Saints won their home game and Vince played well. He knew the travelling time to get from Liverpool to Euston, down to Southampton, then back up country to the camp at Liss. He set off in good time but missed his Southampton train by seconds so took a seat on the next train down south, still with plenty of time to arrive back to compete in the games. Being the only one in his carriage he laid out on the seat and jammed his size tens against the door handle and relaxed knowing it was a long, long haul before he changed trains for Liss. When he awoke the train had stopped and on looking out of the window realised that something was seriously wrong. He and the train were in a railway siding. Jumping down to the tracks, Vince found a workman testing the wheels and to his question, 'Where am I', the workman answered, 'Crewe, mate.'

'Crewe! That's miles from where I should be.' With the workman's help, Vince got onto the correct train and made it to Southampton via Euston, but the train to Liss had departed! A taxi was the only thing between Vince and trouble from the NCO. He jumped into a reliable-looking car and set off for Liss. Half way to Liss the taxi lost a wheel! Despite his heroic efforts the taxi driver's valiant attempt to get Vince back in time failed, well short of time and Vince was given seven days' jankers.

Vince still took part in the regimental games and it was at these games that he literally 'bumped' into Bomber Brown, the 6' 4" North African Heavy Weight Boxing Champion, both men competing in the shot put at the time. The bump ended in a fight, Captain Walker intervened and ordered both men to the gym to settle the matter in the boxing ring.

Vince handled the Bomber with ease; he was no comparison to Phil Edwards with whom Vince sparred regularly. But like all good stories, there is a twist, the Bomber ended up playing rugby for the regimental team and both men became good friends!

Vince served his time as a National Serviceman and came out of the 'mob' as fit as the proverbial 'butcher's dog' and ready to hit the top of the pile in rugby league football.

3

THE BIG TIME AT SAINTS

Vince's all-action style was adored by the Saints' supporters while opposition followers grumpily agreed that 'That young Karalius is a good 'un'. But one particular incident in a crucial Saints v Wigan derby match drew a resounding guffaw of laughter from the spectators, and no one ever laughed at a derby match. Yorkshire man Ron Gelder was the referee on a mud-thickened pitch and after 10 minutes one player looked exactly like another, and the referee too was covered. As Wigan launched an attack, Vince targeted the Wigan player about to take a pass. Bang, in went Vince with all his usual venom, shoulder first. Wham, a bell-ringer. The poor Wiganer crumpled in a heap as the wind was knocked out of him. Oops! Vince found the dangerous Wigan player was Ron Gelder the referee.

'Sorry Mr. Gelder, are you all right sir?' Vince asked. 'Aye lad, is that the best you can do?' said the well-liked referee and everyone, players and crowd alike, had a good giggle about the tackle.

Two weeks after demob Vince played in a 20–12 win up in Whitehaven for Saints but his biggest moment in football was waiting just around the corner.

His first big chance in representative football came when, less than a month after demob, he was selected for a Rugby League XIII to take on the 1955 touring Kiwis at Odsal, Bradford, with the match played under floodlights. In 1955 we were still only a fledgling country regarding TV and sadly our game was a poor relation compared to soccer, cricket and rugby union. But the TV people decided to allow the final twenty minutes to be shown and a cracking game it was. Vince was selected in the second row, in partnership with his old antagonist from his Saints debut, the magnificent Aussie, Harry Bath of Warrington. This selection must have been made with future international selections in mind as any player considered for big games such as this, amongst so many overseas internationals surely came high in the selectors' thoughts.

The strong side to play the Kiwis was: Joe Phillips (Bradford Northern, New Zealand); Brian Bevan (Warrington, Other Nationalities), Duggie Greenall (Saints, Great Britain), Ally Naughton (Warrington, Great Britain), Jack McLean (Bradford Northern, New Zealand); Ray Price (Warrington, Wales, Great Britain), Frank Pitchford (Oldham, Great Britain), John Thorley (Halifax, Wales, Great Britain), Sam Smith (Hunslet, Great Britain), Bob Kelly (Wakefield Trinity, Other Nationalities), Harry Bath (Warrington, Other Nationalities), Vince Karalius (St Helens), Gordon Haynes (Swinton, England).

The Rugby League XIII won an exciting game by 24 points to 11. Vince was outstanding with his enthusiasm and strong defence and his clashes with the big prop Maxwell brought plenty of 'ooh's' from the crowd. During this early stage in his career, Vince could always receive good advice from some of his older teammates. Alan Prescott, Steve Llewellyn, Duggie Greenall, whom Vince swears was the hardest man, pound for pound, that he ever saw, Glyn Moses and Bill Bretherton always had time to talk to the youngster and put him right in his game. All the players at Saints were delighted that things had gone well in his first representative game and the club prepared for the most important period of the season when the road to Wembley stretched out before them.

Vince was cock-ahoop after his rep game and his form mirrored his teammates as Saints went on to some very good wins, although they did suffer defeats, over Christmas 1955 by Leigh at home on 26 December by 11 points to 9, Wigan away on 27 December by 8 points to 0 but had a good Christmas Day win over Oldham by 18 points to 7. The gates for the two home games were 19,000 and 21,000 and the crowd at Central Park was 20,924 – great days for spectators.

The Challenge Cup saw Warrington beaten 15-6 at Saints in round one in a match attended by 23,000 spectators. The following League games were mostly won as Vince and the team maintained a top four place, but it was that smell of Wembley that grew with the second round draw of Castleford at Knowsley Road. Cas were dispatched easily before 15,500 folk by 48 points to 5. Now for the third round draw and the players sat around the radio: 'St. Helens, (hurray), will play, Bradford Northern'. Hats in the air, a cracking chance now.

Bradford were demolished 53–6 in front of 26,000 people. What now for Saints? Before the semi-final the derby match against Wigan at home loomed. This match really gave the Saints team a shot in the arm as Wigan were beaten by 29 points to 7 before 32,000 people. A defeat at home to Warrington possibly showed the pressure of the forthcoming Challenge Cup semi as Saints' opponents were to be the ultra tough Barrow. And in one of the hardest semi-finals seen, the epic struggle ended up as a 5–all draw at Station Road, Swinton in front of 38,897 fans, with the replay called for the following Wednesday. Central Park, Wigan was the venue for the replay and another titanic struggle ensued with the score being 0–0 after 80 minutes. Extra time saw Steve Llewellyn and George Parsons score tries and Austin Rhodes kick two goals in front of 44,731 people, to put Saints at

Wembley against the strong, powerful Halifax side who had beaten Wigan at Bradford by 11 points to 10 before a crowd of 51,889.

Vince suffered a worrying injury in the second semi-final when his ear was almost ripped off. The doctor stitched the wound but the Saints board were not sure if Vince would be fit for the final and had a meeting with Jim Sullivan on the matter. Vince declared himself fit but told Jim Sullivan he did not fancy the idea of wearing a scrum cap as it would draw attention to the injury. Jim said, 'Leave it to me; I'll fix it before the game.'

Saints had a tradition of preparing for big matches by having training sessions at Southport, the lovely seaside town just above Liverpool and an ideal quiet spot to get some serious training done. Saints were ready and particularly Vince who missed Saints' last Challenge Cup Final in 1953 when just making his way in the game. Added to this the Final was a great opportunity to write the record books as Saints had never won the Challenge Cup before in the club's history. The official trip to the Stadium on the day before the match brought back a few memories to Vince as the players walked on the sacred turf. This time, no slip ups! The two teams were evenly matched but traditionally Halifax relied a lot on their big, tough pack, and the Blue and White hooped jerseys made them look bigger somehow. Not only were the Halifax pack feared, their backs boasted some fine players too. The Halifax team up against Saints that Saturday was: 'Tuss' Griffiths at full-back and goal kicker. Both wingmen, Arthur Daniels and Johnny Freeman were Welshmen, as was Griffiths. The two centres, Tommy Lynch a cracking New Zealander and the big Cumbrian, Geoff Palmer, who had power as well as pace in his cupboard. No two finer footballing half-backs could be found anywhere than Ken Dean, a local lad who was an international and county player at stand-off and the Castleford coalminer, Stan Keilty, also a county and England man at scrum-half. Crafty as a box of monkeys and sharp as tacks the pair of them. The dreadnought pack consisted of two Cumbrians, Alvin Ackerley, hooker, and prop John Henderson, a Welshman, big Les Pearce, two Yorkshiremen, Jack Wilkinson, a local lad from Pellam Lane in Halifax and Albert Fearnley who hailed from Clayton in Bradford and one Northumbrian, Ken Traill, although thought of as a Yorkshireman was in fact born in Northumbria and moved as a baby when his dad Jim Traill signed from rugby union for Hunslet. A big, tough mobile pack from which Halifax's strength generated.

The Saints too had a fearsome six with the lead from the captain and Great Britain skipper as well as the Lancashire County captain, Alan Prescott, one of three Widnes-born forwards in the Saints pack, the others being Doug Silcock and Vince. The much travelled Len McIntyre was the experienced hooker and Welshman George Parsons and local lad Roy Robinson a powerful second row pair. The backs had a balanced look with Glyn Moses, a Welshman via Salford, at full-back, the brave, experienced Steve Llewellyn and the very quick Frank Carlton on the wings, Brian Howard and the great Duggie Greenall in the centres and two excellent half-backs in Bill Finnan and goal kicker Austin Rhodes.

- In the dressing rooms at Wembley, Jim Sullivan called Vince over to him. 'Let's have a look at that ear' said the great man. Vince offered the sore ear for inspection but Big Jim gently turned his head and began to tape up Vince's good ear, laminating with 1" Elastoplast. Jim finished the strapping and told Vince to cover the sore ear with Vaseline. 'There we are, they will never notice the bad ear.' Vince remembers vividly taking the first catch of the ball from the kick-off and running the ball back at the Halifax pack which was converging upon him. Although there were almost 80,000 people in the Stadium, everyone cheering and shouting, Vince can still hear the voice of a Halifax forward calling, 'Get his boody ear'. Two Halifax forwards did just that, they tried to grab the ear with the plasters on it and left the sore ear alone. Great thinking by Jim Sullivan.

The game was as tough as could be. Hard running in the forwards, trying to wear each other down but the hard training by master coach, Jim Sullivan, had prepared the Saints well for this final. Vince gave a strong lead, as did Alan Prescott and it was the experienced prop's early tackle on ball handling danger man, Traill that 'cleaned out' the international loose forward and made him a passenger for the remainder of the game. Hard and tough as it was, the teams came in at half time with no score on the scoreboard, 0–0. So it was for most of the game but one could sense that it would take only one slip for the game to be lost. Freeman, the Halifax flyer, was injured when he fell over a photographer on the touchline. With only about fifteen minutes to play, Vince made a half break and off loaded a superb pass to Brian Howard who, in turn provided a perfect pass to Frank Carlton some 70 yards out from the Halifax line. With a bit of space to work in Carlton zoomed away to round Griffiths in brilliant fashion, and holding off the injured Freeman crossed for a dramatic try which was converted by Rhodes.

Now with their tails up, Saints swept on to attack again and Llewellyn darted over and Lance Todd winner Prescott smashed over late on after supporting another crashing Karalius break. And with Rhodes adding another goal Saints only deficit was a Griffiths penalty goal to give Saints the cup for the first time with a 13 points to 2 victory. The big trophy won at last. The first time in Saints history that the grand old Challenge Cup was going to their home!

Vince was delighted, his memories of that 1953 final were

now replaced with a terrific performance by him and a great victory for his club and his mates. He also felt good for his mentor, the man who had guided both Vince and the team to this historic win, coach Jim Sullivan. Not too much can be said of Jim Sullivan's impact on the young Karalius and although mentioning Vince's admiration for Big Jim earlier it is well worth telling again. Since June 1952 Big Jim had nurtured and moulded Vince into a hard, fit, fearless forward. Vince signed for Saints in August 1951, Sully arrived in June of the following year. Sullivan's training was hard and unrelenting. His coaching technique had been honed as a world class full-back whose play and kicking skills were legendary. Coming from Welsh rugby union, Jim won every medal available and toured as a Lion three times, captaining the 1932 side. Jim's only playing club was Wigan and on ending his playing career he was appointed coach at Central Park, winning all the major cups in an unrivalled coaching career. Leaving Wigan was one of the biggest stories for years, young newspaper men earned great reputations because of it but when all was said and done, it was down to money. The Wigan board decided that the winning bonuses, given to him in season 1951-52 would be withdrawn for the following season. Sullivan could not agree to this and joined Saints. His man management was first class, handling backs and forwards alike, temperamental players, youngsters, old stagers and trialists all fell under the spell of this magic coach. In his first season he guided Saints to the 1953 Challenge Cup final against Huddersfield and Vince, as a youngster, was travelling reserve. About this time Vince was knocking 'em cold in the A team and playing really well when 'Sully' drafted him into the first team. He could not understand why Big Jim put him back into the reserves after playing well in the first team, but Big Jim knew! The coach eased him in until the time was right, when Vince had matured in size and strength. No doubt Big Jim smiled when he saw Vince getting bigger and bigger whilst in the army. Then, the number 13 jersey was his. Tactically Sully was brilliant too, remember him taping Vince's good ear for the final? Little things that make great coaches.

The Challenge Cup was presented by that grand old soldier, Field Marshal Earl Alexander of Tunis and the St Helens' supporters did their team proud when the Red and White heroes walked out in front of the Town Hall with the cup. Duggie Greenall got a special cheer as he had been one of the few players at Saints who had gone through the mediocre times at Knowsley Road and had overpowered the big threat from Geoff Palmer at Wembley. Every single member of the St Helens police force was on duty to welcome home the team. The Challenge Cup win rounded off an acceptable season, the Wembley win plus a top four spot in the league was enough to build on and with a visit by the Australian tourists due in September 1956, a Great Britain Test jersey must have been up for grabs for the now experienced, yet still young, Vince Karalius.

4

SUCCESS IN AUSTRALIA

The season 1956-57 started with the usual wins for Saints but the eternal bogey team, Oldham, came to Knowsley Road and ended a five match winning run with a 25 points to 16 victory. Great news for Vince though was his selection for the Lancashire County team to play Cumberland at Wigan in early September 1956. The win by 42 points to 21 did Vince no harm at all as again his ferocious play gave him good reports. The Lancashire Cup opened with a 27-7 win against Swinton at Saints watched by 17,000 people. Round two offered an easier passage when Liverpool City came to Knowsley Road and were beaten 34–3 with a 9,000 gate, and a win at Warrington before a crowd of 26,000 by 17 points to 9 put them into another Lancashire Cup Final to meet the bogey team, Oldham, at Wigan. Before a crowd of 39,544, Oldham continued to be the jinx team when they beat Saints 10–3.

The 1956 Kangaroos arrived, captained by former Leeds hooker, Ken Kearney. It was the third and final tour of the great Aussie full-back, Clive Churchill and the Aussies had a shock when an ordinary Leeds side beat them 18–13 at Headingley. In early October Vince was selected for a test trial and played for the Great Britain side against The Rest. The loose forward for The Rest was Edgar Dawson of York. Vince had another very good game as the Great Britain side won, 26–23 but was disappointed when the selectors went for the in-form Dawson to play loose forward in the first test at Wigan on 17 November 1956. Great Britain won 21–10 on a rain-soaked afternoon.

Another rainy day greeted the second Test at Odsal, Bradford. With Dawson injured, Vince fancied his chances but Derek Turner, who had produced a superb display in the recent Lancashire Cup Final win over Saints, was preferred and the Aussies won by 22 points to 9, with the British pack being dismantled in the process. It was even more irksome to Vince because the weekend before the second test, the Aussies came to Saints and Vince had a blinder in an astonishing 44–2 victory over the tourists. Vince himself rates this victory as one of Saints' best ever performances and so did the critics. Saints' domination up front was emphasised by all the forwards scoring tries, Prescott, McCabe, Terry, Silcock, Gaskell and Karalius crossing the whitewash in great style. Llewellyn with two, Rhodes and Dickinson also scored tries and Rhodes landed seven goals. With the score 18 points to nil at half time, Saints took the much vaunted tourists to the cleaners and could have had more tries with a bit extra luck. In fairness, Marsh, the Balmain second rower, suffered a leg injury and Banks, the quick Toowoomba number 6, came off worst after a clash in one of Duggie Greenall's famous tackles, but the visitors, internationals or not, were decidedly second best on this day. Vince laid down his credentials again to the selectors and they could not ignore his form and reputation much longer. For Saints however, they did not make the top four and the superb win over the Aussie tourists was the highlight of the season.

A bonus for the Karalius family early in 1957 was that Vince's younger brother, Dennis, signed on for Saints. A chip off the old block, Dennis was a tough forward whose junior club had been Widnes St Maries.

The Lancashire Cup came around again and Saints

progressed to the semi-final with wins over Workington Town, away, by 16 points to 12 and Blackpool Borough, away, by 28 points to 12. The semi-final was against the bogey team, Oldham at Knowsley Road and a shock 29-9 win by the Roughyeds sent Saints tumbling out of the competition. What made it harder to swallow was that in August, Saints had gone to the Watersheddings and won in fine style by 21 points to 7.

Six weeks later Saints made one of their best and most important signings in the club's history when they gave a debut to their new South African wingman, the Springbok, Tom Van Vollenhoven, one of the best wingmen to grace our game. Now an unusual thing happened around this time. Vince hit a patch in his game that occurs to every player at some time in his career – he lost a bit of form! This had never happened to him before and he found it hard to come to terms with and could not understand why the breaks were not forthcoming. A few tackles were missed; a pass or two went astray, all the symptoms of a good player losing his form. Trying harder only made things worse and he confided in a good friend and team mate Steve Llewellyn telling him that he was thinking of asking Jim Sullivan for an extended rest. Llewellyn recognised the problem immediately and advised Vince strongly to persevere and play himself out of this bad patch.

At this time the policy of the Rugby Football League was to play tour trial matches before selecting the touring squad and as the 1958 tour was due at the end of the season, all the players were thinking of making those trials, then boarding the plane for Australia and New Zealand. Vince had knocked on the international door for a season or two but his loss of form had come at the wrong time and, so he was left out of the first trial. Llewellyn had said that having played with

Vince at Saints and having spoken to former tourists, he was sure that Vince would make a perfect tourist being tough and fearless. 'Go for it Vince', Llewellyn had said, 'you have all to gain and little to lose.' Vince was selected for the second trial at Headingley on a cold, wintry Wednesday afternoon. He was to be in the Green team to play the Whites. Also in the Greens was that cheeky chappy, Alex Murphy the brilliant young Saints scrum-half who had signed as a youngster from St Austin's in St Helens. The strength of the Great Britain squad can be seen by any devotee of the game when shown the two teams that lined up that snowy afternoon.

Greens: Bateson (Hull FC); Brian Smith (York), Ayres (Oldham), Challinor (Warrington), Wookey (Workington Town); Archer (Workington Town), Murphy (Saints); Herbert (Workington Town). Prior (Leeds), McTigue (Wigan), Huddart (Whitehaven), Martyn (Leigh), Karalius (Saints).

A good side but the Whites were also topped up with great players,

Whites: Fraser (Warrington); Boston (Wigan), Lowdon (Salford), Webster (York), Carlton (Saints); Gabbitas (Hunslet), Fishwick (Rochdale Hornets); Barton (Wigan), Sam Smith (Hunslet), Owen (Leigh), Winslade (Oldham), Shaw (Hunslet), Clifft (Halifax).

Murphy was outstanding at half-back and the young Hunslet stand-off, Gabbitas, was prominent in broken field play but the trio of top forwards were Huddart with his powerful, speedy runs, McTigue a master at slipping the ball away in the tackle and general tough play and Vince with that aggressive defence and quick darts in mid-field. The touring team was selected that weekend and held shocks as three 'certainties' were omitted: Boston (Wigan), Owen (Leigh) and Winslade (Oldham).

The full touring squad was: full-backs: Eric Fraser (Warrington), Glyn Moses (Saints); wingmen: Bill Wookey (Workington Town), Frank Carlton (Saints), Mick Sullivan (Wigan), Ike Southward (Workington Town); centres: Eric Ashton (Wigan), Jim Challinor (Warrington), Alan Davies (Oldham), Phil Jackson (Barrow); stand-offs: Harry Archer (Workington Town), Dave Bolton (Wigan); scrum-halfs: Alex Murphy (Saints), Frank Pitchford (Oldham); Props: Alan Prescott (Saints), Brian McTigue (Wigan), Ken Jackson (Oldham), Ab Terry (Saints); hookers: Tommy Harris (Hull FC), Alvin Ackerley (Halifax); second rowers: Dick Huddart (Whitehaven), Brian Edgar (Workington Town), Mick Martyn (Leigh), Dennis Goodwin (Barrow); loose forwards: Johnny Whiteley (Hull FC), Vince Karalius (Saints).

It is hard to believe now but Vince was not selected in the original tour squad. When the selections were seen by tour manager, Tom Mitchell, he demanded Vince's inclusion and the man to drop out was Brian Edgar, one of Tom Mitchell's own club players from Workington Town. Edgar returned to the squad when the tough Oldham forward, Sid Little, withdrew from the tour. A selector told Mr. Mitchell that Vince was left out because he was 'too hard to handle'. Funny, that's what the Aussies thought!

Vince insists some of the best advice he ever listened to was from Steve Llewellyn when the shrewd Welshman told Vince to keep playing and come through the loss of form without resting!

So it had happened for the tough kid from West Bank juniors, selection as a British Lion on a tour Down Under. Vince now had the chance to show those Aussies what this Widnes kid was made of and he couldn't wait to wear that Great Britain jersey. From his first appearance on tour Vince made his mark against all the top names. His style of all action defence was not the 'head high take a chance' tackling favoured by quite a few players for both Great Britain and Australia in those days. No, Vince would stop a runner dead with anything and everything he had but his favourite tackle and the one which put the wind up the Aussie players and public alike was that special Karalius blockbuster, in which he completely encased the runner with arms, legs and body in a bone-crushing, all-enveloping vice-like crash tackle that stopped man and ball with the ball carrier left with no chance to release a pass to his teammates – Vince simply stopped the movement! The crowds down under hated him, yet loved him too and every red-bloodied Aussie wished that Vince was playing for them.

Western Districts caught the Lions cold in the tourists' fixture out in Orange, where the country boys played above themselves and with a little help from the officials, gained life-long notoriety by gaining a 24 points all draw on the second game of the tour. Newcastle were beaten 35-16, Northern NSW beaten 27-17 at Tamworth, a very strong Sydney side were beaten before 48,692 people in a tough set-to by 20 points to 15 and the tourists beat a tough Riverina rep side in Leeton 29-10. With just one more game before the crucial First Test the Lions were scheduled to take on a test strength New South Wales rep side in Sydney. Now the usual ploy by all Australian administrators was to throw a real humdinger of a hard fixture immediately before the First Test, to soften up the 'Poms', then unleash the full strength test team onto, they hoped, a wounded Lions outfit. Well, the New South Wales representative side sure played to orders, with head high tackles, stiff arm tackles, knees in the double tackle and what later became known in Australia as the 'gang tackle', involving several tacklers holding up the ball carrier and an extra couple coming in to 'clout' the standing and already held opponent. These New South Wales v Lions games were traditionally rough, tough matches with no quarter given or asked. In the previous 1954 Lions tour, this same fixture was abandoned after 56 minutes and all twenty-six players were sent off for fighting by the Aussie referee, Mr Aubrey Oxford, in a game in which Vince's great chum Duggie Greenall took no prisoners whatsoever. But the match in 1958 was just as tough and although the Lions won 19 points to 10 an incident occurred which showed the darker side of the Aussies' sporting mentality.

Early in the game, Vince had clobbered big Doug Camaron in a one-on-one tackle and the Aussies didn't like it one bit. Referee, Col Pearce, pulled out Vince and Lions captain, Alan Prescott to officially warn Vince about his aggressive defence but after that it was open season on Vince and one or two other good Lions players. Peter Dimond, the big tough Aussie centre/wingman, and a player renowned for his short fuse and ability to look after himself, clashed with Vince. The result was that Vince was sent off for an action he had never done in his football career, kicking an opponent. Vince will tell to this day that yes, he did hit Dimond with his Sunday punch and that Dimond fell to earth as though shot, out cold. Col Pearce said 'off' and pointed to the dressing room. Vince walked, to the boos and jeers of the Aussies, most of whom loved this no-nonsense Pom loose forward. The crowd of 52,963 didn't have long to wait for a procession of players who received their marching orders and all were Australians. Second rower, Rex Mossop, who also played for Leigh, walked for hitting Eric Ashton off the ball, stand-off Greg Hawick for kneeing Phil Jackson and Vince's mate Peter Dimond left the field for an early bath for lashing out with his boot at Mick Sullivan.

The opinion was that 'sending off sufficient' would be the verdict of the New South Wales Judiciary Committee when they met straight after the match at the Sydney Cricket Ground. But the verdict was, 'Mossop, one match, Hawick and Dimond suspended for ten days and Karalius will be judged in two days time'. What a shock, Vince was suspended for 15 days! Dimond had been dismissed for blatantly kicking at Mick Sullivan and received only one match suspension. Vince insisted, so did several other players, that he did not kick Dimond but even then, his suspension encompassed three games. The Aussies had realised the impact Vince had brought to the British team and did not want him in that vital First Test match.

It was obvious too that the Aussie players had targeted Vince for an early bath by provoking him during the game but the incident with Dimond upset the tough forward as he knew that kicking an opponent was not his style and never had been, yet this trumped-up charge had made him miss the First Test and the next two games also, against the very strong Brisbane rep side and the tough Queensland State side, both games being in Brisbane.

The Aussie newspapers had a field day with Vince being a crowd pleaser and a crowd baiter. They picked up on Vince liking classical music and without doubt the Aussie journos are the worlds best at sniffing out a nickname or latching onto something that 'sticks'. His all action, no-nonsense style of play squeezed out some of their best work as amongst the lots of publicity Vince received were these 'classics' that matched his music, and I quote these Aussie comments from *Lucky Thirteen*: 'This Karalius believes there is no room for "I beg your pardon" in football' … 'Karalius, by his vigour and octopus like tackles, does everything to stir the blood of his opponents, this mobile forward is one of the most destructive players that England has ever sent to Australia' … 'A fine footballer, Karalius is a bit hot headed' (meaning they couldn't handle him!) 'but he gave both half backs a torrid day, bowling them over before they could even move' … 'Vince Karalius, the Wild Bull of the Pampas, is a dedicated destroyer of Australian forwards' … 'The boiler-maker with classical tastes in music can stiff arm to the lilt of Il Trovatore' …. 'As he clocks the Aussie forwards he probably hums the Toreador song from Carmen.'

In a nutshell, they bloody loved him!

The First Test was approached in fairly confident mood and a side good enough to win the game was selected. The Lions that day were: Fraser; Southward, Jackson, Davies, Sullivan; Bolton, Murphy; Terry, Harris, Prescott, Martyn, Edgar, Whiteley. A side good enough to beat anyone if they played well! The problem was that they didn't play well. The Aussies would not allow them to play well. The Aussie administrators did as much as their players in winning this test match. Statements were issued by the Aussie press accusing the Brits of over-aggressive play amongst the forwards and the over-enthusiastic use of the stiff arm tackle by almost all of the Lions team. The inconsistent referee, Mr Darcy Lawler, demanded a pre-match discussion with the Lions and warned that he would 'walk' anyone attacking with a stiff arm. It was 'clean play' or else. Clean play? Alan Davies was knocked out by a stiff arm when hooked off his feet and Dave Bolton was punched in the face as he attempted to round the Aussie full-back, Newtown's Gordon Clifford. Stern lectures from Mr. Lawler were the outcome of these deliberate fouls as the Lions continued to play as though all the fire had gone out of them and they played with a 'don't upset anybody' attitude. This does not win test matches and it lost this First

Test by 25 points to 8. A terrible blow to the Lions' confidence but a modicum of blame should be levelled at the Lions' management team as they should have stood up to the Aussies and not looked for the easy way out. Selection too, with the omission of Huddart and McTigue, did not help the Brits' cause plus the unavailability of Vince on that trumped-up charge meant that half the Lions strongest pack were sat on their backsides watching the test match. 68,777 folk watched the slaughter of our test team and almost all of them must have rubbed their hands at the thought of a drubbing being on the cards for the Lions.

From Sydney the squad moved up north for the Queensland leg of the tour and Brisbane were beaten 34-29, then the State team were beaten by 36 points to 19. After that the Lions went on an orgy of scoring against the slightly weaker Queensland opposition. Central Queensland at Rockhampton were demolished 61–19, Wide Bay at Bundaberg by 50 points to 25, Far North Queensland at beautiful Cairns 78–8 and North Queensland at Townsville 78–17. The next game was the most crucial match of the whole tour as to lose it would mean disaster in that the Ashes would be lost.

The decision to take the test squad to prepare at Surfers Paradise was a master stroke but no one could ever guess at the dramatic history making game or the near lasting fame that awaited those thirteen Lions on that sunny afternoon in Brisbane when, even the most biased Aussie cane cutter, with the slouch hat, a pack of 4X and a tattoo of Don Bradman on his chest, couldn't help but give a begrudging 'well played' to those Lions in Brisbane.

In our game's long and exceptionally brave history, no happening can ever compare with the incomparable 'Rorkes Drift Test', named after the vastly outnumbered

British soldiers who held out against thousands of Zulu warriors in that hospital station in South Africa in January 1879. Being made to play three test matches in eight days in 1914, the Lions were reduced, by injury, to ten men for most of the second half, yet hung on to a slight lead and in fact won the test, 14–6 and the series by two tests to one. The captain was the 'Prince of Centres', Harold Wagstaff of Huddersfield, and this game and its legend has been handed down from generation to generation as the epitome of bravery and national pride. But if any game can be placed alongside the 'Rorkes Drift Test' for bravery and absolute doggedness of spirit, this Second Test in Brisbane in 1958 may well compare. The game was Vince's test debut. The thirteen heroes were: Fraser; Southward, Ashton, Challinor, Sullivan; Bolton, Murphy; Prescott, Harris, McTigue, Huddart, Whiteley, Karalius. After four minutes Alan Prescott broke his arm and was so badly hurt that he was advised to leave the field, but refused, so important was the victory required by the Lions. Shortly after the Prescott injury, Dave Bolton suffered a fractured collar bone and was forced to leave the battle. Karalius, Fraser and Challinor were all taken to hospital after the game, because of injuries. The Lions were badly depleted. Folklore has it that at only the fourth scrum, the Lions hooker, Tommy Harris of Hull FC appealed to Prescott, 'The scrums are loose skipper', to which the hero captain replied, 'Sorry Tom but I have broken my arm but we'll say nowt about it now though'.

In agonising pain, Prescott was about to go off for treatment when Dave Bolton went down. The skipper decided to stay on the field with his teammates and with Vince now in the unfamiliar role of stand-off half and forming a very strange looking half-back partnership with his Saints buddy, Alex Murphy, the heroic tourists battled it out.

'Murph', at 19 years old and at the time the youngest ever player to tour, showed unbelievable maturity as he tore the Aussies apart with electric bursts in mid-field. Keith Holman, the brilliant Aussie scrum-half, who played directly opposite Murph just could not control this young superb upstart. With the strong running Cumbrian, Ike Southward, notching two tries and the ever reliable Mick Sullivan and excellent footballer, Jim Challinor one each, to go with Eric Fraser's four goals, the half-time decision by the captain to stay on the field despite the doctor's warning about the possible consequences, was justified. Vince, playing with a badly bruised spine, Eric Fraser battling on with burst blood vessels and a badly strained elbow and Jim Challinor carrying a severely damaged shoulder would all have been brought off in a normal game but this was not a normal game and no doubt, had Bolton's injury been anything except the crippling collar bone fracture, he too would have demanded to be allowed to play on.

Leading by 20 points to 7, against probably the strongest side the Aussies had produced for a few years: Clifford, Kite, Hawick, Carlson, Dimond, Brown, Holman, Davies, Kearney, Marsh, Mossop, Provan and O'Shea, the Lions looked to have run out of steam as the Kangaroos hit back with tries by Carlson and Dimond to go with Bill Marsh's try and Clifford's two goals which reduced the margin to 20 points to 13 with still plenty of time left. But the injury-ravaged Lions held out and in the closing stages, some 30 yards out from the Aussie try line, a little Saints set-piece worked wonders. Harris won the ball from the tight and Murphy picked up and shot, like a bullet, to the open side, Vince trailed him in true loose forward style, even though he was at stand-off, and Alex hit the supporting Karalius with the pass. Vince charged on and when the Aussie cover was about to swamp the injured Lion under several tacklers, he found Murphy with a return pass and the unbelievably quick scrum-half was in the clear and as Alex would say, 'It was goodnight nurse'. Away he flashed, like lightning, no Aussie on earth could catch him and with Fraser's fifth goal it took the score to 25 points to 13 with only minutes left. Holman did manage to crash over and Clifford kicked the conversion to make the historic final score, 25 points to 18, and thirteen heroes names went into the pages of history that day.

The enormity of the win, not by the score but by its emotional greatness, took British rugby league onto a different plane. The Aussies were shell-shocked at the way the Poms had stuck it out against uncountable odds. They should have given up when confronted by those severe injuries. 'How, with so many key men injured, did they manage to hold out, let alone win?' asked one newspaperman. Well, I suppose now, looking back, the words willpower, guts, determination, sheer unquestionable bravery and bloody good players spring to mind.

But there was another test to play and the series was tied at one all. The tourists made their way back down to Sydney by way of Toowoomba, where they beat the local side 36–19, then on to Lismore where North Coast were beaten 56–15. The big city on the south-east coast was waiting for the brave men of the Brisbane test win. Alan Prescott and David Bolton, sadly, took no further part in the tour but, after treatment, the captain stayed on until after the test series. The big decider was played, as usual, at the Sydney Cricket Ground and, in a way, this match too would go down as a 'special' test match.

Enforced changes saw Alan Davies, the excellent, tough, Oldham centre come in for the still injured, Jim Challinor. Big Phil Jackson deputised for David Bolton at stand-off and

Ab Terry took the place of his club and country captain, Alan Prescott, at open side prop. Fraser and Karalius had recovered enough to take their places in a still strong-looking side. Controversy set in from the moment the referee was appointed. Jack Casey, the top whistler from Queensland, was given the hardest job for years in Australia. Unlike the finicky Darcy Lawler, whose obsession with clean and not too rough play made no allowances for test match rugby league, or the unpredictable Col Pearce, who controlled a game acting like gelignite, no one knowing when he would explode into making a crucial mistake, against either side, Aussies or Brits, Casey was a straight shooter and gave what he saw and considered right at the time. Because Jack Casey was a Queenslander he was considered too inexperienced to take a huge match such as this and the New South Wales biased crowd of 68,720 souls let it be known just how they felt. Changes to the Aussie test team from the embarrassing Brisbane defeat had to happen and Ian Moir, the South Sydney flying wingman was recalled, so too the great Harry Wells of Western Suburbs, back into the centres whilst Greg Hawick moved to stand-off to replace Tony Brown, of Newtown.

The success of taking the Great Britain test squad away to Surfers Paradise after the First Test nudged the management into a similar move and before the match the test squad moved out to the beautiful area of Cronulla, where the surf is supposed to be the best in New South Wales and the beach is outstandingly picturesque.

So the teams paraded for the national anthems and it was in another very warm environment that the game started. Phil Jackson skippered the Lions in Alan Prescott's absence and it was obvious, in the early stages that the Aussies were hell bent on knocking the 'Poms' out of their confident stride. The first half was very close and tries by Southward and Terry, plus four goals by Fraser gave the Lions a narrow 14 points to 12 margin as Holman and Provan had registered tries and Clifford had kicked three goals. The second half brought scenes of aggressive discontent amongst the Aussie crowd as referee Casey awarded two penalties on the trot to the Lions. From the second one, Murphy suddenly spotted an opening and was through it in a breath, veering away from the cover and leaving them for dead, the superb young half-back turned Clifford inside out as he scorched to the line for a wonderfully memorable try. Shortly after, Mick Sullivan swooped over and Fraser converted to give the Lions a 22–12 lead. The Aussies were beside themselves, catcalling Casey at his every move and it was obvious that the game was on a knife edge as to whether or not the crowd would invade the pitch. The next sensation made it very possible as the Aussies rallied and but for tremendous defence by Huddart, Whiteley and Vince, they would have added to their score. The speedy Moir was unleashed by Wells and as he approached Fraser, chipped over the Lions full-back and looked all on a scorer but was apparently obstructed by Southward. Moir stumbled but regained his feet and chased after the ball at great speed and dived over the try line but failed to ground the ball which was picked up by Eric Fraser and he transferred the ball to Mick Sullivan who ran the length of the field to score a devastating try. Absolute mayhem broke loose. Missiles were aimed at referee Casey, bottles, stones, oranges, anything that came to hand was hurled onto the pitch. Boos and catcalls were shouted at Casey as calls for an 'obstruction try' were refused by the referee who was adamant that Sullivan's try should stand, and stand it did. As the debris poured onto the field and the Lions players realised that the try would stand, some of them had a bit of fun with the crowd. It started when a couple of

British players waved back to the booing crowd which caused even more catcalls. One player picked up a bottle of beer and pretended to drink it, this brought a laugh from some of the crowd and when another player picked up an orange, peeled it and started eating it some of the fired-up Aussie spectators saw the funny side and actually applauded the player. All the players helped to clear the playing area and the test match restarted but the Aussies were broken, the heart had been wrenched from them and the Lions grew with each moment. One or two typical test match flare-ups occurred as Keith Holman squared up to Vince and the pair went at it for a while, then Brian McTigue, a strong, teak-tough forward had a ding-dong with big Norm Provan bang in front of Mr Casey but the referee let it go as it was a test match and rightly so.

The test match and, above all, the Ashes were won in a most emphatic manner with the try scorers, Sullivan – a majestic hat trick, Terry, Southward, Murphy, Alan Davies and Johnny Whiteley and eight superb goals from Eric Fraser. The Aussies had Provan, Holman and Hawick to thank for their tries and Clifford kicked four good goals. The injured captain, Alan Prescott, arm in a sling and happy as a sandboy, was the first onto the field to congratulate his players and Vince, Mick Sullivan and Phil Jackson chaired the skipper off amid joyous celebrations. Prescott paid compliments to all the side but had a special word for Vince and Brian McTigue. 'Of all our players Brian and Vince were the stars of a great pack performance. Vince Karalius has been a key man for us in the last two tests and I can't praise his play highly enough.'

The trip across the Tasman Sea to New Zealand was a happy one. The major part of the job was done but the cagy, hard-to-beat on their own ground Kiwis were no pushovers. The first obstacle was against the fierce Maoris in Huntley. The Lions registered a fine win 59–7, then it was the First Test in Auckland. The Lions selected a strong test line-up with pace a-plenty in the backs and a big, mobile pack. The side was, Fraser, Carlton, Ashton Davies, Sullivan, Jackson, Pitchford, McTigue, Ackerley, Goodwin, Huddart, Whiteley and Karalius. The Kiwis also selected from strength and on a rain-sodden pitch on a rain-swept afternoon the Kiwis had on duty, Eastlake, Hadfield, Griffiths, Turner, Denton, Menzies, Roberts, Ratima, Butterfield, Maxwell, Johnson, Kilkelly and Percy.

With Tommy Harris out of the side it broke a tradition going back over 50 years. Until this current Kiwi test, no Lions touring side had taken the field without a Welshman in it and it turned out to be a bad omen as the New Zealanders, playing almost perfect wet weather football beat the odds on favourites by 15 points to 10. Sullivan and Jackson touched down for tries and Fraser kicked two goals whist for the Kiwis, Percy with two, and Hadfield scored tries and Eastlake added three goals. It came as a shock to their systems but it had to be faced, the Lions played well below themselves but the home side had played exceptionally well.

In the 'district' games, the Lions really went to town to prove that the First Test performance was a one-off. Taranaki at New Plymouth were slaughtered 67–8, Sullivan crossing for six tries, and Wellington in the 'Windy' City, were beaten 62–20. Canterbury in Christchurch put up a better show but went the same way to a 41–21 defeat. The tough coal miners from the West Coast at Greymouth did well to hold the tourists to a 19–2 result and the final 'district' game gave the Lions their biggest ever win in New Zealand over North Island at Palmerston North by 72 points to 3. All set for the final test of the 1958 tour back in Auckland. The Kiwis, naturally, were unchanged but the Lions had Jim Challinor back for Alan Davies, Davies at stand-off for Phil Jackson, Alex Murphy in for Frank Pitchford, Tommy Harris in for Alvin Ackerley, Brian Edgar in for Dennis Goodwin and Goodwin in for Johnny Whiteley. It was a different display by the Lions this time when Sullivan scored a hat-trick of touchdowns with Ashton, two, and Murphy following him over for tries and Fraser kicking seven goals. The Kiwis answered with Hadfield, Roberts and Percy scoring tries and Eastlake kicking three goals to give the Lions a 32 points to 15 victory. The attendance at the second test was 25,000.

One further fixture was played in New Zealand when the hard tackling Auckland rep team were beaten 24–17 in Auckland before a meagre 5,000 spectators. The Lions then returned to Australia to play three final games against New South Wales Colts in Sydney which the Lions won 19–11, New South Wales Coalfields in Maitland again the Lions were successful 30–23 and a long flight across country to Perth to play Western Australia and win 69–23. Mick Sullivan scored a record 38 tries on the tour and Mick Martyn scored a record 23 tries for a forward. A superb tour on the playing side ended with that game in Perth but repercussions were just around the corner when once at home. It was on this tour that Vince struck up a long term friendship with his room-mate on tour and forward partner in many future Saints successes, Dick Huddart the then Whitehaven second rower, soon to join Vince at Knowsley Road.

5

RETURN FROM OZ, MARRIAGE AND SAINTS

The brilliant 1958 Lions touring team flew home in August 1958 bringing with them the Ashes, a tour to remember all their lives and, unfortunately, memories of sometimes bitter battles on occasions between players and management. It had been an historic tour, full of on-field bravery, acts deserving of a medal in war time and a tour that, as most did, developed a camaraderie second to none and to the highest level of good fellowship. A record breaking tour too, Mick Sullivan set up a new tour try-scoring record and Eric Fraser kicked 110 goals. The bravery aspect was of course the Second Test at Brisbane when the tour skipper, Alan Prescott, wrote himself into the heroes book of rugby league folklore with his courageous decision to play on with that badly broken arm and the other injured 'troops' who so gamely carried on to everlasting glory with that great victory. The tour also discovered one Vincent Karalius as a fearsome opponent of the begrudging Australians. Begrudging because the Brisbane test, won by the Brits against all the odds, was Vince's test debut and his overall fierceness in every game in which he played gave birth to the now eternal nickname of 'the Wild Bull of the Pampas'.

When delving into Vince's psyche regarding his outlook and mental preparation for each game, one must remember how immensely built up for each physical encounter he became, his 'hate campaign', his determination to win and his natural aggressive attitude against any opponent, hence the Aussies, although historically used to a legion of tough, hard Pommy loose forwards, were completely dumbfounded when confronted by this 'Wild Bull' in that tremendous Brisbane win.

The tour was a financial success with the surplus being in excess of £50,000 and each player earning around £600 bonus for the trip but the stigma of those early problems influenced the Rugby League Council to instigate a five man committee to look into the problems and prepare a secret report on the squabbles of the tour. So secret was the meeting that it was held behind closed doors. The committee pencilled in to meet on Monday, 15 December 1958 under the chairmanship of the respected Chairman of the Council, Mr F Ridgway (Oldham).

Meanwhile, Vince's season got under way for Saints on 8 September 1958 in the 12 points to 2 hard-fought win in the Lancashire Cup second round against Leigh at Hilton Park and he settled back into the everyday working, training and playing routine that was his life – although there was now a young lady in this life, Barbara Pilkington.

Saints had started the season in good style even though they lost against Widnes in the first game at Naughton Park by 25 points to 15. They progressed in the Lancashire Cup by beating Rochdale Hornets at the Athletic Ground in round one by 20 points to 15 on 30 August 1958 and in the league, after the Widnes defeat, gained victories over Rochdale Hornets away, Featherstone Rovers and Warrington at home and Wakefield Trinity away before Vince came back in the win at Leigh. The month of

September was a busy one for Vince. Not only was he committed to his club and just back from an exhausting three months tour but he was recalled, after a two season lay-off, to support the Lancashire County team effort to win the prestigious County Championship. Vince had an outstanding game in the huge win against Cumberland at Wigan by 60 points to 12 on 10 September, two days after the Leigh win. On 13 September, Vince was back in action in the 45 points to 20 win over Halifax at Knowsley Road, then in the Lancashire Cup semi-final at Saints on 17 September in an 18–6 win against Barrow and finally, off to Hull Kingston Rovers ground, Craven Park, to play Yorkshire on 24 September only to loose heavily by 35 points to 19. Five games in 16 days including a hard cup tie, a semi-final and two County Championship matches. The 'easy' game was against the fearsome Halifax who never, ever took any prisoners. The County Championship play-off was Lancashire v Yorkshire at Hilton Park, Leigh and was a thriller. Another top game by Vince could not stop a 16 points to 15 win for the White Rose against the old enemy. This inter county play-off took place only four days after a big disappointment for Vince when Saints were beaten in the Lancashire Cup Final by arch nemesis Oldham at Swinton by 12 points to 2. So again, so near yet so far as two major medals were lost in four days but in club football no one would guess that Saints would go unbeaten after the Oldham defeat in the County Cup final until the first week in January 1959.

A feature of the game in Vince's day were the fixtures over the holiday periods. For instance over Christmas 1958, Saints and Vince played Leigh, away, on Christmas Day and won a tough encounter by 10 points to 6 before 13,000 spectators. On Boxing Day Wigan were the visitors to Knowsley Road and Saints won by 13 points to 9, phew, another close one, in front of 32,000 and the day after, 27 December, 28,000 watched Saints beat Oldham 22 to 6 at home! Three hard, rough games in three days with 73,000 in total seeing the one at Leigh and the two at Saints – some men, some crowds, some games!

It was around this time that the five man Rugby League Council committee met, on Monday, 15 December 1958, to discuss and formulate a report on the unacceptable goings-on that occurred on the very successful tour in the summer of 1958. Vince and Dick Huddart had been involved in one incident, being late in after curfew, but lots of incidents were reported to do with the general running and organisation of training, food, over-the-top discipline for grown men and various other indiscretions from both players and staff management. The entire Rugby League Council had been disturbed by the rumour and innuendo that had drifted back to England from the touring party. The three staff, Mr Manson, Mr Mitchell and coach Jim Brough, were invited to give their side of things but other than the five Council members and the three tourist bosses, the meeting was supposed to be private, in fact 'in camera'. But it is well known that very little can ever be 'secret' in rugby league. Someone always finds out somehow! To be fair to the five man committee, the actual minutes of the meeting have never been publicly opened up to journalists, the details that we do know have come from other sources, employees at RLHQ and the like. Mr Manson was accused of wrongdoings in certain areas of the tour and Jim Brough had a percentage of his tour bonus withheld because of the way he conducted his coaching duties and caused a little upset because of his too strong line of discipline amongst the tourists. The main criticism of Mr Mitchell by the committee was the selection of Jim Brough as tour coach as he knew that Brough may well cause friction amongst certain players and that he, Mitchell, may not see eye to eye with Brough's draconian regime, yet he made no mention of his fears to anyone until after the tour. Brough of course was the Workington Town coach at the time of selection for the Lions tour and Mr Tom Mitchell was in fact a leading member of Workington Town's board of directors, hence the tour manager's fear.

What was strange was that the problems that arose on the 1958 tour should be highlighted four months after the return of the tour party and particularly after a hugely successful tour both on the field and through the turnstiles. Vince, in his book, *Lucky Thirteen* explains, 'On a tour of such importance and magnitude, it is obvious that Mr Manson, Mr Mitchell and Jim Brough would sometimes have to wield the big stick and by doing so, made themselves unpopular at times. But in their defence they had been sent on a 30,000 mile round trip to put football before everything.'

Swinton director, Bennett Manson was the business manager on tour and taking an article from a national daily newspaper of the time, it stated that '...Manson, on more than one occasion was called out of his bed to stop the 'horse-play' by some of the tourists in his hotel late at night'. One thing seems to be clear, the rounds of parties and late night stop-outs were being abused by some of the tourists and after the hammering in the First Test something had to be done as the lack of discipline was showing through into games. One knows that a certain 'perk' of touring is the new people one meets, new ideas one picks up and being given a peek into a lifestyle an ordinary working class lad never sees.

But having a peek and taking it on board as one's own lifestyle is not acceptable to a rugby league Lion. To Jim Brough's credit he did confess to a member of the travelling press that, 'If Mitchell will give me fifteen players and let me take them away we will win the Second Test', hence the special training at Surfers Paradise – and the rest is history!

Despite Jim Brough doing the chores that a coach did on those past tours, like being on call to see to the kit-skip and administer to sick and injured players (most unlike today), he had to face charges of breaking his contract because of speaking privately to the press, refusing to massage players and being absent from the hotel when he was required to treat the players. One reason for the upset was that Brough had no set rota for his duties and players expected him to be at their beck and call, whereas if working to a rota system, he would have legitimate time for himself. Vince admits a certain amount of 'horse-play' amongst some of the tourists. In all fairness, when is there not horse-play when twenty-six fit, young men are together on tour? The old favourite pastime of letting fire extinguishers off came into play in one particular hotel, but it was possibly not high jinks, more a cry for someone to listen to the players' grievances. The food situation at this hotel was not right. Brough had instructed the players that they were eating too much meat and it would be cut down. The players insisted that it was the vegetables that were scarce and that surely they knew their own diets and what did them good prior to a game. A 'clear the air' discussion was called and the point of criticism was aimed at Mr Manson and Jim Brough for having too much of a 'sergeant major' attitude to discipline. The players won the battle on this point and normal meals were resumed, with plenty of vegetables!

But the biggest problem for the management staff was when the tourists had moved across the Tasman Sea on the New Zealand leg of their tour and Jim Brough again introduced his curfew. Feeling betrayed after the glorious results in Australia, the whole team signed a 'round robin' letter and sent it to the Rugby League Council in England, declaring a vote of no confidence in coach Jim Brough. Right or wrong? There were points for and against doing it. The 'round robin' had been written when the tourists were in Wellington, having lost the First Test in Auckland only a week before so there may have been a feeling of 'sorry for ourselves' about the decision, anyway the letter was sent and this, above all, may have moved the Rugby League Council to action.

Vince and the Saints went on a winning spree until early January 1959 when they were beaten narrowly at Headingley by Leeds, 12 points to 11 and twenty-one days later returned to the City of Leeds to take on a revitalised Hunslet at Parkside where Saints were beaten by 19 points to 11. The Knowsley Road outfit were an excellent side, brim full of internationals with power and pace, but such was the nature of the game then that the unexpected happened more times than today, when virtually any team on their day could beat any other team, if they hit form. This Hunslet team though were having a great season and Vince and his pack mates found it heavy going against a side made up of mainly young, local lads, with experience in the right places.

Then on 14 March Vince was again back in Leeds for his home international debut when he turned out at Headingley in Great Britain's big defeat of France by 50 points to 15. Back in club football, Barrow were slaughtered 71–15 at Saints. Then the team removed the hiccup in a cracking

Challenge Cup win at Oldham, by the odd point in 13, in the first round, followed by a big win in the second round against Dewsbury, 35–8. Vince and his teammates were now steaming towards Wembley but the club had a tricky third rounder against Featherstone Rovers at the graveyard of most good sides, Post Office Road. Once again the dreaded voodoo struck as the Blue and White shirted warriors from Featherstone won a memorable contest by 20 points to 6.

A week later, calamity, a trip to Central Park and a defeat by the old enemy, 19 points to 14. The Saints were well placed in the league table but to ensure a home game in the Championship semi-final Vince knew that few slip-ups could be tolerated with the Championship the only trophy left to win to show something for this consistent season. A further loss at Swinton by 19 points to 11 made them sweat but a final flourish of wins gave them a home semi-final against Oldham.

Saints went to the Watersheddings only one week before the semi-final to meet Oldham in the last league match of the season and lost the game by 15 points to 14, a week later the Roughyeds came to Knowsley Road feeling confident because of the previous week's good win over Saints. No slip-ups this time as a very strong St Helens side gave Oldham a lesson in fast, open football supported by a strong, virile pack of forwards who paved the way with strong support play. Ken Large scored a hat trick of tries and the magical Alex Murphy was in great form as the Saints tore Oldham to pieces in a magnificent 42 points to 4 victory to gain adequate revenge for the final defeat in the Lancashire Cup earlier in the season.

Two weeks later the Saints had to travel to the huge Odsal Stadium, the natural bowl that could hold well over 100,000 spectators as it did for the replayed 1954 Challenge Cup final. This Championship final was eagerly waited for as the unsung Hunslet team were quite capable of causing an upset as proved with the Yorkshire side's victory back in January 1959. Vince and his men were determined this time though that the Championship trophy was coming back to Lancashire to sit in the Saints trophy cabinet for the next year. The crowd was about half of the 1954 world record at 50,569 on that sunny afternoon of 16 May 1959 as the brave Hunslet side of local lads fought all the way against a very skilful and speedy Saints side.

Hunslet's team on the day was: Langton, Walker, Stockdill, Preece, Collins, Gabbitas, Doyle, Hatfield, Smith, Eyre, Gunney, Poole and Shaw. St Helens fielded an experienced side, full of international players: Rhodes, Vollenhoven, Greenall, McGinn, Prinsloo, Smith, Murphy, Terry, McKinney, Prescott, Briggs, Huddart and Karalius.

The game was said to be one of the most enjoyable, good open football games ever seen in a Championship final. Hunslet started up like world beaters and soon ran in a 12 points to 4 lead but a wonderful try by Saints' South African wingman, Tom Van Vollenhoven, turned the game on its head. Receiving the ball some 75 yards out from the Hunslet try line, Vollenhoven, with a series of side steps, swerves and out and out pace, beat five would-be tacklers in his surge to the line. Brave Hunslet played their part in this show-piece game by continuing to play expansive rugby, throwing the ball from wing to wing and stretching the Saints defence in which Vince had an outstanding game. But the pace of Vollenhoven, Prinsloo, Huddart and Murphy was just too much for the heroic team from South Leeds. The score of Saints 44, Hunslet 22 shows the speed at which this game was played. For Saints, Vollenhoven registered an outstanding hat trick of tries, Murphy chipped in with two more and other individual try scorers were Huddart, Wilf Smith and Prinsloo. Rhodes kicked ten glorious goals. Hunslet's scorers were Doyle, Stockdill, Gunney and Poole and Billy Langton landed five goals. This wonderful win was tinged with sadness though. Vince's mentor and the Saints superb coach, the great Jim Sullivan, decided to leave Saints and take the contract option open to him to leave one year before his contract terminated. He joined Rochdale Hornets as senior coach on a five-year contract starting in the 1959-60 season. It was goodbye not only to a coach, but to a friend, he would be missed by the players he transformed.

On 4 June 1959, Vince married Barbara Pilkington. Vince, who always calls his good lady by the nickname, 'Pilky', first met Barbara in 1958 when Vince was looking around to buy a pub and run it as landlord. He had a friend who owned a pub in Sutton Leach, The Wheatsheaf, and had arranged to call in to have a look at the workings of licensed premises. Barbara was working, part time, behind the bar and that is how the couple met. Barbara's dad, Harold, was a shrewd business man and encouraged Vince to consider various commercial ideas and to work for himself as his own boss. Since finishing his National Service, Vince had worked at a well known local firm, McKecknies, and since his rise to international level as a rugby league player had very much fancied making the most of his fame and turning his well known persona into a successful commercial venture. Harold, his father-in-law, gave Vince some sound advice, 'Start up for yourself lad, you'll never make much working for someone else'. Well Vince did and in 1960 Vince and his brother Dennis took the plunge and started up. But before that Vince was called into international duty to play the French in 1959 and got into hot water again, this time being caught, red handed, having a quiet drink with his best buddy, Dick Huddart by team boss Bill Fallowfield.

The test series against the touring Aussie 1959-60 team saw the First Test at Swinton. Included were only two players who did not tour in 1958, Billy Boston and Derek Turner. Vince was omitted and on the day that Great Britain were beaten 22 points to 14, Vince was playing up in Whitehaven in a weakened Saints team because of test calls, yet won well by 15 points to 12. In the Second Test Turner was left out for the return of Johnny Whiteley, Don Robinson came in for Dick Huddart and Jeff Stevenson replaced Alex Murphy and in an exciting encounter, the Brits won a thriller by 11 points to 10. Whiteley retained the Number 13 jersey for the third and deciding test at Wigan and Britain won 18–12.

One wonders if the problems of the 1958 touring team and the breaking of the curfew, plus the being caught drinking by Bill Fallowfield had any significance in the fact of Vince's non-selection so soon after the successful tour? But the club scene at Saints saw a good start to the Lancashire Cup with a win at Station Road over Swinton by 17 points to 9. Then a 24–9 win at Naughton Park, Widnes, gave Saints a semi-final place at Whitehaven. Vince played in the first two rounds but then missed almost a month through injury, in fact Vince only played in nine games for the remainder of that season from the win at Widnes in the Lancashire Cup. An 18–2 win at Whitehaven put Saints into the final against Warrington at Wigan. The 'Wire' won the trophy with a closely fought, hard game by 5 points to 4, before a crowd of 39,237. Three weeks before the final, the touring Aussies, remembering the drubbing they received four years earlier, won at Knowsley Road by a rousing 15 points to 2, filling them full of confidence with the victory over the British champions.

About this time Vince had found out from Harold Pilkington, his father-in-law, that two good wagons and a contract to cart bricks was being sold off and that the deal was a bargain. Vince went with Harold to see the wagons and they both needed a lot of work doing on them. Now Vince's father-in-law was registered blind and Vince to this day has a smile when he tells of going to look at a pair of wagons with a man who was blind, and the same man had recommended them! Vince bought the vehicles and converted them both into tippers, with his skill as a blacksmith/welder. Dennis, Vince's brother, joined him in the venture and the family business empire bloomed from that. Then the welding side took off and a scrap business began. From that, they purchased a fifty per cent share in the Nelson Northwest Hotel Group and a great platform of commerce was gradually formed within the Karalius set-up. It was hard graft for all the family, long days but Vince still had his rugby to act as a safety valve where he could let off steam. Barbara and Vince's personal family grew too as two girls and a son were born, Diane, Stella and little Vincent who, God rest his soul, died only days old. The Reverend Vincent, Vince's catholic priest uncle, officiated at little Vincent's funeral. Stella and Diane prospered, Diane now lives on Grand Canaria and Stella and her husband Ben, both doctors, reside with their four children on the Isle of Man along with Diane's daughter Gemma who lives with Barbara and Vince. Gemma, who is a great all-round sportswoman is a sport science graduate and has a practice specialising in the treatment of sports injuries.

The 1960-61 season started for Saints with Alex Murphy asking for a transfer, Austin Rhodes relinquishing the club captaincy and Vince out injured. Luckily all those problems were resolved and the new season brought a well-deserved recall to international rugby for Vince when he was included in the Great Britain v The Rest in a trial for the World Cup squad to take on Australia, France and New Zealand in the third World Cup competition which was to be played in Britain. Great Britain had won the first in France, and Australia had won the second 'down under'. But having developed the habit of arriving as late as possible, to avoid the sitting around before matches, Vince missed the trial because of arriving too late. This trial team was designed to put together three of the best ever British back row forwards in the same pack, Karalius, Whiteley and Turner. Fortunately Vince's slip-up was overlooked and the Great Britain squad included him and he played in all three matches as the British strength and toughness again proved a winner.

Played in a league system, Great Britain beat New Zealand 23–8 at Odsal, and France 33–7 at Swinton. Australia scraped through by 13 points to 12 against France at Wigan and fought a hard battle to beat New Zealand 21–15 at Headingley. But the big game was Great Britain against Australia at Odsal, the winners of which would lift the trophy. In a gigantic end-to-end brawl that became known as 'the Battle of Odsal' the game was a 'pay-back' by most of the players for previous actions against them and fist fights took place every few minutes, sometimes as many as eight players a time were brawling and one fight in the second half involved all the 26 men on the field. One report in the local newspaper told of an Australian forward being catapulted out of a set scrum by one fierce punch, another floored by a knee into his face! The result on that mud covered Odsal pitch was a win for Great Britain, with tries from Boston and Sullivan and two Fraser goals to a Brian Carlson try for the Aussies, which gave Great Britain the trophy.

Nine British clubs had players in the successful winning squad, Fraser, Challinor and R Greenough (Warrington), Jobie Shaw (Hallifax), Ashton, Sullivan and McTigue (Wigan), Brian Shaw (Hunslet), Frank Myler (Widnes), Alan Davies (Oldham), Jack Wilkinson, Derek Turner (Wakefield Trinity), Harris and Whiteley (Hull FC), Murphy, Rhodes and Karalius (Saints).

Vince then retained his international place for the test match against France at Knowsley Road in January 1961 where Great Britain won by 27 points to 8 in front of 18,000 spectators.

On the domestic front, success had come early for Vince in the Lancashire Cup when wins over Widnes, away, in round one, by 19 points to 17 – Vince missing this one – was followed by a typical local derby, at home against Wigan with a gate of over 30,000, by 7 points to 4. Vince had returned for the Wigan game and for the semi-final at Leigh when Saints battled to a 15–2 victory. The Lancashire Cup Final was played before a crowd of 31,725 at Wigan against the very dangerous Swinton outfit, Saints coming home with the beautiful trophy by 15 points to 9.

The season went well in the league and Saints finished in the top four which earned them a trip to Headingley in the Championship semi-final. With a bigger game the week after it wasn't too surprising that Saints lost this semi-final 11–4 against Leeds. The Challenge Cup was the target though and what a cup run Saints had. A scare in the first round when neighbours Widnes came to Knowsley Road and fought out a creditable 5–all draw. The gate at Saints was 14,617 but at Naughton Park in the replay it was a huge 24,205. Saints did not allow lightning to strike twice and with Vince in the lead, the Saints pack dominated to win the replay by 29 points to 10. Vince was now captain of the side and the hero of Brisbane 1958, Alan Prescott, was coach. Rumours arose in the club that the Saints board of directors were thinking about bringing in Jim Brough, the coach of the 1958 tour. The players felt that it would be disastrous as one or two had not seen eye to eye with him on tour, besides, all the players thought the world of Alan Prescott and they figured that it would not be long before there would be a change of club coach should Brough arrive. But the rumours died down as the team continued its march towards Wembley. Castleford were drawn in round two, away, and Saints took on the hard Yorkshire side, who always took some beating 'down t'lane', as they say in Cas. But another fine forward display, plus tries by Vollenhoven, Alex Murphy and two from the recently signed Mick Sullivan, added to the three goals by Austin Rhodes in a tough 18 to 10 win gave Saints a leg-up in the competition to play Swinton at home in the crucial third round. Brian McGinn, Alex Murphy and Dick Huddart romped over for tries and Austin Rhodes kicked four goals in a 17–9 win.

The side was now through to the Challenge Cup semi-final and the draw took them to play Hull FC in the huge Odsal bowl. The other semi-final was between Wigan and Halifax at Swinton. Vince missed the Hull semi-final because of a torn medial ligament but into the side came a big, strapping Londoner, who had answered an advert in the

Sporting Chronicle for good, big, strong rugby union forwards. He certainly was that, as he developed into one of the all time great British prop forwards, Cliff Watson. Cliff had come north from Kingswinford rugby union club and was just 21 years old when he burst onto the big stage. Hull FC knew the way to Wembley. They had been for the previous two years, beaten by Wigan in 1959, then twelve months later in 1960, beaten heavily by the excellent Wakefield Trinity. The men from the Boulevard were confident, although their renowned pack of forwards though were not the outstanding force of three years earlier and using their faster backs, Saints won easier than people thought. 26 points to 9 was the score and all Saints tries came from their star-studded backs, Rhodes, Vollenhoven, McGinn, Large and Wilf Smith with two, whilst Rhodes landed four goals, before 43,000 spectators.

Over at Station Road, Swinton, Wigan overcame Halifax by 19 points to 10 to set up the dream Wembley final, Saints v Wigan, and what a final! Vince would be back for that one but despite winning well, the crucial games to force the team to the top of the table were lost. All thoughts now were directed at the old enemy, Wigan. People in the north-west counties had, for many years, hoped for this classic final. The traditional style of football played by both these wonderful sides built up an image that should they ever meet at Wembley, then a feast of superb football would take place on that glorious green acre. But suddenly all the glitz and glamour of Wembley was forgotten as the rumours rose up again regarding Jim Brough assisting 'Precky' at Saints. Vince and his men picked up that the board had met with Brough already and this was the final straw. With Alan Prescott's future in mind, the players had a meeting and one of the members typed out a letter addressed to the Board of Directors. In it were the thoughts of all the players at the club. It was a letter of deep sympathy for 'Precky' and a no-nonsense vote of no confidence in Jim Brough. Signed by all the international players and the youngsters the letter was also a warning of the sentiments of the players so very near the biggest game at the club since 1956. The wise directors decided 'not to pursue the matter further' and the players made a strong point that no one was wanted at the club who would be a threat to the much respected Alan 'Precky' Prescott. But no one at the club could ever have realised that Alan's days were numbered even though the club was on the verge of a stupendous victory involving their near neighbours and arch enemies, Wigan.

The date rolled around and Saints had their traditional Southport training sessions and the side was in great spirits as they set out for their date with destiny. The day dawned bright and sunny as both coaches settled their judgements on the two teams and the starting line ups were, St Helens: Rhodes; Vollenhoven, Large, McGinn, Sullivan; Smith, Murphy; Terry, Dagnall, Watson, Vines, Huddart, Karalius. Wigan; Griffiths; Boston, Ashton, Bootle, Carlton; Bolton, Entwistle; Barton, Sayer, McTigue, Collier, Lyon, Evans. The referee was Mr T W Watkinson (Manchester).

The heat inside the Empire Stadium, at ground level, was intense. 94,672 people were crammed into the ground. As Vince proudly lead out his Saints team to be presented to the Earl of Derby and other dignitaries, turned across the half-way line and headed towards the Royal Box stand, he thought just how close he had come to ending his football career to concentrate on the business that was going so well for himself and his brothers, Dennis and Terry. If anyone expected a classic game they would have been disappointed. It was a hard, no quarter asked nor given, local derby, with tackling as fierce as any test match and in this phase of the game no one was more prominent than Cliff Watson.

In overpowering heat the two teams fought out a see-saw contest of strength. It was a test of wills, which team would surrender in the blistering heat? Huddart went striding clear from an astute Karalius pass, up on the big Cumbrian's shoulder zoomed will-o-the-wisp Alex Murphy and over he flew for Rhodes to goal. Wigan's reply was two good penalty goals by South African full-back 'Punchy' Griffiths. At the start of the second half Wigan threw everything at the Saints line and wave after wave of attacks crashed into the Saints' defensive wall. Boston went to the line only to be crunched in a brilliant Watson tackle, McTigue was held on the line by Watson and Vince, Carlton was 'boot-laced' by Watson when apparently clear to the line. It was hectic, nail-biting and phenomenally exciting as Griffiths hit the post with a penalty kick and the ball bounced out. Then suddenly there was a magic moment in Challenge Cup history. Deep inside his own quarter, Vince spotted a weakness on Wigan's left hand side. Instead of running the ball into the Wigan forwards, he hit a wide pass to Ken Large who found a huge gap in front of him as he broke clear. Large veered to his right and found the speedy Vollenhoven coming like an express train. Vollenhoven took the pass and went away down the touchline, Griffiths had his fellow South African covered and Vollenhoven was very close to the touchline as the big full-back moved in to the tackle. Suddenly Large was on the inside of his wingman in perfect support, Griffiths made his move on Vollenhoven who passed inside to Large. But now happened an incident that is still discussed when rugby league men meet – Griffiths committed the cardinal sin of not taking Vollenhoven out and into touch as he passed to Large. The centre accepted Vollenhoven's pass and sprinted away, chased all the time by Eric Ashton. Only yards from the line the heroic Ashton caught the flying Large but Vollenhoven had run out of play at Griffiths' challenge and sprinted onto the inside of Large. As Ashton hit Large with a glorious leg tackle, the Saints man flicked an inside pass to his partner who ran around under the posts for the most exciting try ever seen at Wembley. But why, oh why did Griffiths allow Vollenhoven to run on after his inside pass to Large? If the Wigan full-back had tackled the Saints wingman then Vollenhoven would not have been there to take Large's pass to score! One of the many mysteries of Wembley.

Griffiths added a penalty goal to make the final score, 12–6 with Dick Huddart picking up the Lance Todd Trophy as the best player of the match. The players and board celebrated in the Russell Hotel in London. Everything looked rosy, the Lancashire Cup and the Challenge Cup in the cupboard, key players still gaining international selection, the club had money in the bank and a fanatical support both home and away. The reception in St Helens when the team arrived back with the cup was equally as enthusiastic as the first one in 1956. Over twenty thousand fans clamoured and shouted for the players as they paraded on the Town Hall steps. Vince thanked them all for their support and many encouraging words were spoken as the town went wild with the joy of success. The usual promises of 'We'll be back next year' and genuine good wishes from the supporters came over thick and fast and a feeling of good will spread over the club and its followers.

Vince missed the start of the 1961-62 season. He was finding the training, that he had always done so intently, was eating into the time that he should be giving to his business. He was also feeling the strain of the knee injuries and bumps and bruises that he had accumulated over the long years of giving everything in his play. But he was back to lead Saints into the Lancashire Cup Final, again at Wigan against Swinton in front of a crowd of 30,000. The result was a great victory by 25 points to 9. Then in October 1961, Saints played host to the touring Kiwis and in keeping with results against touring sides beat them convincingly, 25–10. Granted this Kiwi team was not the strongest to visit these shores having played 20, won 8 and lost 12, but they were still an international touring side.

Going into December 1961, only seven months since he had led out his team at Wembley, Vince was in the doghouse again. On 9 December Saints had an away game at Wakefield Trinity and as usual the team was to travel by train. Now, as we have described, Vince was not one to sit in the dressing rooms for an hour before matches, nor was he one to sit in the railway station waiting for late comers to arrive, so he cut things fine. He would arrive dead on time so that he would spend as little time mooching around as possible. This day he got his train times mixed up and arrived at the station to find the board, the team and the train gone! He had missed it by minutes. He dashed outside the station and grabbed a taxi. Every traffic light, every snarl up, every tractor to get behind was against, in front of and behind then all the way to Wakefield. Remember that there was no motorway then and all the roads were single lane tracks with slow moving lorries and private cars.

Vince was greeted by ice cold faces and attitudes when he

finally reached Belle Vue. He knew that there would be words said at the next board meeting and he knew that he may be in for a telling off from the chairman, Mr Harry Cook. To compound Vince's misery, Saints were beaten by Wakefield which took them to four defeats in five games – not at all what Saints were used to. No, the Board had to do something and quickly. As soon as the team arrived back in St Helens, it was announced that the captaincy had been taken away from Vince and given to Alex Murphy. Mr Cook made the best of a sad job but as he said, 'Vince is not being victimised but the team captain must set an example. We could not just ignore this and pretend it did not happen. Anyone else that kicks over the traces will be in trouble too.' Alex Murphy said at the time, 'I am pleased but I wish it had come in different circumstances. Vince is one of my best friends and if ever the club want to give it back to Vince, I will willingly give it up.'

Two weeks later, Alan Prescott was sacked as coach. Terribly hurt by it, he was 'stunned' as Vince says in *Lucky Thirteen*, 'He went straight home to bed and his wife told me that he is upset Vince and blames the defeats at Wakefield and Oldham'. A statement from the club said that the St Helens board had terminated the appointment of Mr Prescott as coach, that Mr Stanley McCormick would take temporary charge of coaching duties and the financial side of Mr Prescott's agreement had been completed to the end of the season.

A few days into the New Year of 1962, Saints bought Bill Major from Widnes and it was obvious that he had come to play at loose forward. The board moved quickly too in signing new blood as on the day they sacked 'Precky', they paid £8,000 for John Temby, Whitehaven's big second rower, who was a converted centre. All this trouble caused Vince to once again contemplate retiring from the game to concentrate on the booming business with his brothers. On top of his debating retirement or not, Vince could not come to grips with the silly rumours that were circulating around St Helens about his not caring for the club and how he had become selfish and awkward amongst his teammates. One story buzzing around for twelve months or more was that Vince had punched a great pal of his, one of the team, in the face and broken his nose before a cup tie, in the dressing room. In a lovely turn of phrase, Vince describes his feelings at the time of this trouble, 'I could devote more time to our scrap business as Saints were putting me on a slow train to the scrap heap'.

On 19 January 1962 Saints put Vince Karalius on the transfer list at £8,000. He was still only 29 years of age, an age at which there was still a lot left in the tank. This was a loose forward of tremendous international standing, a man the Aussies were petrified of. He had joined Saints as a kid, a youngster. In his wildest dreams Vince would never have thought of leaving Saints but as the welding shop got busier and busier and he could spend more time with Barbara, he suddenly realised that he was gradually getting the brilliant club Saints out of his system. Super, wonderful Saints, of the white strip with the bright red band, he thought sometimes of the mates he had, of Jim Sullivan and Dick Huddart, of going to Wembley and winning the Lancashire Cup, of the scintillating Van Vollenhoven and the sparkling, effervescent, cheeky Alex Murphy and all the others who made his eleven-year stay at Knowsley Road so successful. Vince also thought of just lately how he had missed a few training sessions and cried off a couple of matches, this wasn't Vince Karalius. But the the enthusiasm was dwindling and the fires were going out, was this the end in rugby league for the great man? Not on your life, he returned with a vengeance.

In March 1962, Widnes, his home town team, paid Saints the princely sum of £4,500 and with it, stoked the fires up in Vince again. Vince accepts that apart from his last few months at Saints, it was a huge wrench for him to leave. He calls Saints, the 'Everton of Lancashire rugby league' and that is a compliment. But in going to Widnes, Vince knew that what he was doing was what he wanted – to be back in the game which owed him so much and to which he owed so much. In a way, joining Widnes was like returning home as his cousin, the great Frank Myler, was resident there as captain of the side (Frank would emulate Vince in 1970 when he would captain a successful touring side in Australia and bring back the Ashes.) The coach too was a household name, Joe Egan, former captain and hooker of Wigan, Lancashire, England and Great Britain, one of the all time greats and a devotee of Vince's mentor, the great Jim Sullivan. Joe had played successfully under Big Jim at Central Park for quite a few seasons. So everything seemed set for a great return to football for Vince.

I borrow from *Lucky Thirteen* to put in Vince's own words about how he felt, deep down about his leaving Knowsley Road. 'I felt angry, and a bit disappointed. I wasn't as heartbroken as Alan Prescott when he was told that his services were no longer required at Saints. Alan took it very badly after all those seasons he had given the club as it had been a big chunk out of his life. I had no moans about how Saints had treated me in my youth and in my heyday. I had some good pay days there and there were plenty with many league and cup successes. My anger faded and I felt that maybe I could have played my cards a little better at Saints in those final two or three months that I was at the club. The two reasons that I had only played in a few games by mid January 1962 for the club were injury and business commitments. If I had anyone working for me who didn't pull his weight then I would finish him. That's how the club worked it out and they finished me, no problem but I would defend the fact that I never gave anything except my best when playing for Saints therefore giving value for money to the Saints supporters. Going to Widnes I knew that I would have to pull my socks up as Widnes were giving me a second chance and were pinning their faith in me. I had to make my mind up, which comes first, my new club or my business. After all it was my playing football that made it possible for me to do well in business in the first place. Widnes were treating me generously, the team was good enough to be in the top three in the league under the coaching of Joe Egan and the captaincy of my cousin, Frank Myler and my game was about back to its peak.'

6

WIDNES, WEMBLEY AND BUSINESS

Vince made his debut for Widnes on 17 March 1962 in the home win over Barrow by 20 points to 18. Playing in front of him, in the Widnes second row was his old mate from Saints, Jim Measures, who would himself become a Great Britain forward in the 1963 test series against the Australians. The week after, Vince returned to Knowsley Road to play against his old teammates St Helens and received a rousing reception as he took the field. The result went against Widnes by a narrow 13 points to 8. Vince played the next eight consecutive games to end his first season at Naughton Park completing a playing record for the season of played 10, won 8, the second defeat coming in the game against Oldham at the Watersheddings by 17 points to 9. A good start at his new club.

The season 1962-63 saw the end of the old one divisional system in professional rugby league and in its place was found a new two division set up. The idea had been tried years before, in the early days of the Northern Union but as various teams dropped out of the leagues it was considered that one division was the answer. Times, and the game, had changed dramatically since then and a honed down league of stronger clubs was seen as the way forward. 1962 was also the year of a dreadful winter in the United Kingdom, not so much snow but ice with freezing nights and bitterly cold days.

The season kicked off as usual in August and as autumn turned to winter the Siberian weather took hold and the country shivered to a halt. Widnes were nicknamed, 'The Chemics', because of the vast ICI chemical works and the industry's subsidiary factories in the town. So when the anti-freeze chemical GL5 was made available to the Widnes club and with the well-known referee, Mr Charlie Appleton, being the representative of the firm putting the chemical on the market, and helping to supervise its application onto the Naughton Park pitch, miracle upon miracle, the pitch was soft enough to allow a cup tie to be played on it. On 9 February 1963, Widnes let Liverpool City play their Challenge Cup tie against the Barrow junior club, Roose.

Earlier in 1962, in March, the month that Vince moved to Widnes, the touring team for the 1962 tour of Australia and New Zealand was named. Vince had missed most of the important build-up to selection but such had been his success four years earlier, and success again in the 1960 World Cup, that he thought he had a faint chance of making his second trip 'down under', but no. A few of the great 1958 side made it but as usual several 'certainties' missed out, Ken Gowers, Swinton's excellent full back, former Oldham tried and tested old war horse, Alan Davies, now the Wigan centre, and Frank Myler, Widnes captain and superb stand-off were just three of the casualties. The full squad was: Eric Fraser (Warrington), Gerry Round (Wakefield Trinity); Billy Boston (Wigan), Frank Carlton (Wigan), Mick Sullivan (Saints), Ike southward (Workington Town); Eric Ashton (Wigan) cap, Neil Fox (Wakefield Trinity), Peter Small (Castleford), Garry Cooper (Featherstone Rovers); David Bolton (Wigan), Harold Poynton (Wakefield Trinity); Alex Murphy (Saints), Don Fox (Featherstone Rovers); Jack

Wilkinson (Wakefield trinity), Brian McTigue (Wigan), Norman Herbert (Workington Town), Ken Noble (Huddersfield); John 'Joby' Shaw (Halifax), Bill Sayer (Wigan); Dick Huddart (Saints), Laurie Gilfedder (Warrington), Brian Edgar (Workington Town), John Taylor (Hull Kingston Rovers); Roy Evans (Wigan), Derek Turner (Wakefield Trinity).

The first section of players left by air on a chilly 15 May and the remainder after the Championship Final on 19 May. Although two of the three tests were won in Australia, both tests were lost in New Zealand, which took a bit of gloss off the results. Frank Browne, a leading Australian sports writer, analysing the British tourists, penned an article which is included in *Lucky Thirteen'*. 'Wot, no Vince' read the heading, 'Last Thursday the British selectors named twenty-six players who will tread the path paved by Harold Wagstaff back in 1910. On behalf of those people whose fervent wish is that we repeat our efforts of 1950 and 1954, I wish to move a heartfelt vote of thanks to the said selectors. They did not pick Karalius. They say Karalius has slipped. Whether this man of blood has slipped or not, his absence is the best news that Australia could hear. The robust Vincent created a one man reign of terror the last time he visited these shores. Although we selected our biggest, toughest forwards for that final test, long before half time he had broken most of them from lions to lambs. I don't remember seeing anything as demoralised as that 1958 pack of Australian forwards and the principal demoraliser was Vincent Karalius, a fast moving mass of bone and muscle, with an attitude that would have aroused the admiration of Attila the Hun. In not sending Karalius, Britain has imposed a handicap on its tourists'. Some praise indeed from an Aussie, but very well deserved.

Vince missed the first game in the new competition, the

Western Division, which was introduced as an early season Lancashire League type of trophy, to make up for the deficit of missed league games with having a much reduced full league. The Yorkshire sides played in an Eastern Division. The new first division had only 16 teams participating, whilst the second division operated with 14 teams. Rochdale Hornets, away, were the first Western Division opponents for Widnes and a good win by 22 points to 5 was the outcome. Vince missed only two of the first 13 games of which only two, Barrow, away, by 12 points to 9, and Swinton, away, in the Lancashire Cup, by 5 points to 2, were lost. In the new Western Division, Widnes went through to a final play-off with Workington Town and fought out a 9–all draw, then lost the replay 10–nil. But the majority of the league games went well, apart from losing 25 points to 2 at home and 14 points to 6 away, to Saints! These two league results cancelled out the superbly exciting 10 points to 9 win at Knowsley Road earlier in the Western Division game that really kick started Vince's season. Double victories over Wigan and Leeds were great wins as the Karalius presence began to tell but a double loss to Swinton late in the season cost Widnes a clear second place behind the Station Road side in the final league table.

Widnes finished in third place, on the same 39 points as Saints but with a worse scoring average and both were below Swinton who had 45 points. But it was a rugged Challenge Cup run that really set the stall for Widnes. A tough fixture in round one at Swinton saw a titanic struggle in a 6–all draw. The replay at Widnes ended in a 3–all draw and the second replay ended in the narrowest of wins for Widnes by 6 points to 4, courtesy of three Randall penalty goals. The unbelievable sequence of games in March is worth mentioning as Widnes played the first Cup game at Swinton,

6–all, on the 6th, then Hull FC at home in the league, winning 15-10, on the 9th, the first replay against Swinton, 3 apiece, on the 11th, the second replay, a 6-4 win, on the 13th, then the second round tie against Workington Town on the 16th with a 5 points to nil win giving a total of five games in eleven days. Earn their money or what? But the unenviable cup run ended in round three when Hull Kingston Rovers won at Naughton Park by 10 points to 7.

Vince had been recalled, after a three year break, to the Lancashire County side when, on 12 September, 1962 he played against Cumberland at Widnes in the Red Rose win by 28 points to 8. The second inter-county game was against Yorkshire on 26 September, 1962, at Wakefield and another win by 22 points to 8 to give Lancashire the inter-county championship. A credit to Vince's fitness was that this 1962-63 season had been one of the most hectic periods in his whole career and, including all cup ties, County call ups and all league matches, Vince only missed three matches in all. Added to his daily business commitments, his constitution must have been that of an ox!

In the new season, 1963-64, the format of the Western and Eastern Divisions was changed. Instead of playing all the competition at the beginning of the season as in the previous one, the games were spread and intermixed within the full season's league programme. The Australians were over again on tour in 1963 and this time Vince clashed with the old enemy again both for Widnes and Lancashire County.

A win at home against Featherstone Rovers, 11–9, was followed by consecutive defeats to Wigan, away, and Hull FC at Naughton Park and an early exit out of the Lancashire Cup by Oldham, away, by 10 points to 5 constituted a disappointing start after the good season enjoyed in 1962-63.

Vince gained selection to the Lancashire County side

again and on 11 September 1963, beat Yorkshire 45–20 at Saints, and in a real tough, biff bang match at Wigan, beat the touring Aussies by 13 points to 11 on 25 September. The County Championship hinged on the Cumberland v Lancashire game at Whitehaven on 2 October 1963 when Cumberland took the championship with a strong 13 points to 8 victory over a team in which Vince again had a top game.

On 21 November Widnes played the Australian touring side and despite a spirited display, went down by 20 points to 9. The Widnes side that day was, Randall; Mort, Briers, Thompson, Heyes; Lowe, G. Smith; Hurstfield, Kemel, E. Bate, Argent, Measures and Vince Karalius. Randall landed three goals and Measures scored the try. The fast running Measures was, in fact, the top try scorer in this season with 20 touchdowns, many of them showing the pace, skilful running and evasive qualities of this excellent back row forward.

Forgetting actual league results, playing Widnes in the Challenge Cup at this time was a daunting task. In 1962-63, one only had to look at what a hard, unrelenting job it was to get a result when playing the boys in the Black and White banded jerseys. The original draw against Swinton, then two further replays, allowed Swinton to score a total of only thirteen points in 240 minutes of football, whilst Widnes ground out only fifteen! That's how hard it was to beat Widnes. So the glorious Challenge Cup run in the 1963-64 season must have seemed like déjà vu as Leigh were drawn in round one, on 8 February 1964, and drew at Hilton Park, 2 apiece. The Replay at Widnes was on 12 February and the sides shared 22 points. The second replay was a cracker as had been the previous two and resulted in a Widnes win by 14 points to 2 on 17 February. Add onto those cup games, Salford in the Western Division, on the 15th and Keighley in the league, on the 22nd and that totals up to another five games in fifteen days! Vince missed the three Leigh cup games but was back, in the second row, for the Keighley game and the second round win against Liverpool City by 16-6. The third round tie, against those tough fighters, Swinton, went to another unbelievable two replays. The third round tie, at Widnes, ended at 5 all. The first replay at Swinton finished a numbing 0-0. The second replay was won by Widnes, by 15 points to 3. Vince played in all three of the Swinton games.

Although Widnes have always been noted for their tenacious spirit, in one fairly recent era they were known as the 'Cup Kings', and the tradition of filling the side with local lads helped considerably in making this 'home spun' side almost invincible in big matches. The signing of Vince Karalius was a master stroke whilst still operating in this 'local lad' mode. Vince came to Naughton Park as a world class player, a name renown both here and overseas, a big game, big name player but he also came as a no-nonsense, straight up and down, Widnes lad. He states himself that he came to Widnes and buckled down to his old tried and tested, hard, tough training regime. And his well-known unmovable attitude to the game and his winning psyche brought a new dimension to an already iron hard will to win that was at Widnes.

The League and Western Division games trundled on and the draw for the Challenge Cup semi-final was made. The four clubs involved were Widnes, Oldham – who had never appeared at Wembley – Castleford – the tough mining team from the Yorkshire coalfields – and Hull Kingston Rovers – known as the 'Robins' because of the famous club colours of all white jersey, with a broad red band across chest and arms. The Humberside club had also knocked Widnes out of the competition last season. The draw was made and Widnes pulled Castleford. The game was to be played at Swinton and on the same day, Hull Kingston Rovers would play Oldham at Headingley.

As was becoming the norm, Widnes drew 7–all with Castleford and the replay was at Wakefield Trinity's Belle Vue ground the following Wednesday. Another close game ensued but two Randall goals and a Thompson try saw Widnes home in a breathtaking 7 points to 5 win. It could have been called 'the Widnes syndrome' as the other two semi-finalists drew at Leeds 5 all. Their replay was at Swinton and brought about a game that entered the club's folklore. I have heard all sorts of tales as to why this game ended so dramatically, but being a romantic at heart I like to believe this version. The game at Station Road was an evening kick-off. At the end of the game, it was 14 points all. Extra time of 15 minutes each way was begun but with Oldham leading, 17–14 the referee abandoned the game for bad light. Now I have spoken to a few people who were there and they all insist that a steam train came into Swinton Station and as its steam escaped from the engine, it settled across the Station Road ground. The referee abandoned the game but seconds later the 'fog' lifted and the game was playable, Oldham obviously felt aggrieved but their chance of Wembley was snatched from them. The second replay was at Fartown, Huddersfield, and the Rovers of Hull won through by 12 points to 2.

Now this would be Widnes's fifth trip to Wembley. Twice as winners and twice as losers with this one to come. Hull KR on the other hand were on their first trip to the twin towers although they had twice before made it to the final but they were both played at Leeds, before Wembley became the Mecca of club football. Widnes had last been some fourteen

Vince (far left) meets his hero, Jim Sullivan, for the first time.

Vince and Steve Llewellyn get to grips with Stan Keilty of Halifax.

A Challenge Cup replay v Barrow. Note the crowd for a Wednesday afternoon at Wigan's Central Park.

Albert Fearnley checks the tackle on Frank Carlton as Vince looks on in the 1956 Challenge Cup Final at Wembley.

Joy after the 1956 Challenge Cup Final victory over Halifax by 13 points to 2.

1957 and another great Saints side with Vollenhoven (back row, fourth from left) and Murphy (front row, centre) added. Vince is on the front row, far left.

Vince on the charge against Halifax.

Vince at work and doing great business.

The pre tour trial match before selecting the 1958 touring squad and Bill Wooky (Workington Town) is about to nail Billy Boston (Wigan) with Vince covering across.

The brothers Karalius. Left to right: Denis, Vince, Terence and Laurence.

The Saints team with the very good Ray Price on the front row (second from left).

The super 1958 touring party.

Sydney Cricket Ground, v New South Wales on the 1958 tour. Peter Dimond hits the deck as Vince proves it was not a kick, although it felt like one.

The second 'Rorkes Drift' test programme.

Vince on the move against the Aussies, showing his running power.

Flare up in the World Cup, Swinton 1960. Vince puts away Jean Barthe of France with Brian Shaw, Johnny Whiteley, Brian McTigue and John 'Jobey' Shaw covering Vince's back.

The Saints team following their victory in the 1961 Lancashire Cup over Swinton at Central Park.

Walking out at Wembley in 1961 to take on the old enemy, Wigan.

Vince stopping Billy Boston from the back in the 1961 Challenge Cup Final.

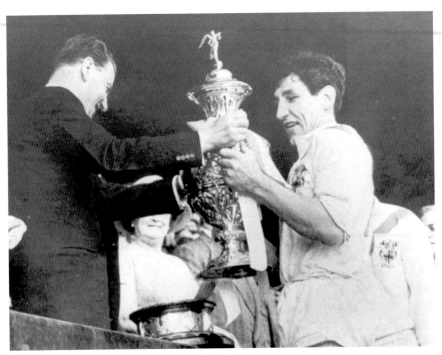

Vince receiving the cup from the Earl of Derby.

Great times after the 12 points to 6 win over Wigan.

Vince, with Dick Huddart (12) and Cliff Watson (10) show the cup to the Saints supporters.

St Helens with the Challenge Cup and Lancashire Cup in 1961.

Vince in his pomp: strong, tough and skilful.

Vince, now with Widnes, introduces himself to Johnny Freeman of Halifax.

On the attack for Widnes against former club St Helens.

'We're on our way to Wembley.' A happy Widnes dressing room after the 1975 Semi Final win over Wakefield Trinity at Odsal with Vince as coach.

Vince and captain Doug Lawton held aloft with the cup.

Cup winners together, Jim Mills and Vince.

'Pilki', Mrs Barbara Karalius, nee Pilkington.

Doing the sand dance with Harry Dawson and building a great family team spirit at Widnes.

Vince and his daughters, Stella right, and Diane, centre.

Back again at Wembley to play Wigan and win 19 points to 6 in 1984 with Eric Hughes as captain and Chairman, Tom Smith.

Vince and Jim Mills with Tom Mitchell, Vince's touring manager in 1958.

Vince with Harry Cook, Tom Van Vollenhoven and Alex Murphy at Vince's inauguration into the Saints Hall of Fame in 1990.

years before to be beaten by near neighbours Warrington, 19–0, but Vince knew the road and knew what it took to lift the cup.

The Cup Final date was 9 May and there was enough experience amongst the Widnes key players, Vince, Frank Myler, Frank Collier and Jim Measures to help the younger and less experienced in big games players from getting too nervous. A solid, tried and tested team was selected for the big occasion and having a sound and unpretentious preparation for the final, they set off for London in great spirit, one or two joking that a draw would do them so they would get more good money from the replay!

84,488 turned out at Wembley to watch this revitalised 'Chemics' team play the quiet achievers from Craven Park, whose team was: Kellett; Paul, Major, Elliott, Blackmore; Burwell, Bunting; Tyson, Flanagan, Mennell, Palmer, Clark, Poole. The Widnes team that day was: Randall; Chisnall, Briers, Myler, Thompson; Lowe, Owen; Hurstfield, Kemel, Collier, Measures, Hughes, Karalius.

The result was a credit to all at the club but especially to Vince, Frank Myler and Frank Collier. Vince had tasted the sweet victories with Saints, Frank Collier had gone three times with Wigan, winning once, losing twice and Frank Myler had served Widnes with distinction but had yet to savour that Wembley feeling. Widnes brought the cup back to Naughton Park with a crushing 13 points to 5 win, Alan Briers registered the first try from a break and superb pass from Vince, Frank Myler and Frank Collier adding a try each and Randall, as reliable as ever, kicking two goals. Frank Collier won the Lance Todd Trophy and the popular Wigan lad was mighty pleased indeed.

A great reception was awaiting the Widnes squad on arrival back home. The club had arrived at a point in its history that would bear fruit in the next decade and beyond.

The strange fixture set-up had Widnes playing Hull Kingston Rovers home and away in the last two weekends of the season. A win by 14 points to 9 at home was followed by a defeat by 22 points to 17 at Craven Park in the final game.

During the 1963-64 season the test series was lost to the Australians by two tests to one. The selectors picked Vince in the first two. Vince had regained his top club form with the Widnes side and was a genuine choice but went into that test with three of the pack who were not up to the rigours of test football. The result was that the Australians cut up the Brits and won the test which was played on 16 October 1963 on the wide open spaces of Wembley, which again suited the Aussies. Reg Gasnier 3, Ken Thornett, Ken Irvine and Graeme Langlands scored tries and Langlands kicked five goals. Our only reply was a Neil Fox penalty goal in a 28 points to 2 drubbing.

The second test was played at Swinton, another huge ground, on 9 November and seven changes were made. Out went Bill Burgess, Norman Field, Dave Bolton, Ken Bowman, John Temby, Bill Sayer and Brian Tyson. In came Mick Sullivan, Johnny Stopford, Frank Myler, Ron Morgan, Cliff Watson, Len McIntyre and Bill Robinson. The only players to play in both were, Ken Gowers, Eric Ashton, Neil Fox, Alex Murphy, Jim Measures and Vince. The Aussies gave us another lesson in open, supporting football and won by 50 points to 12. The saddest part was that this test saw the end of some very famous test careers: Mick Sullivan, Eric Ashton, Vince Karalius and the grossly unlucky Jim Measures who only played twice for Great Britain despite his tremendous ability. It was a sad end for men held in high esteem throughout the rugby league playing world. Vince's Lancashire County career ended too in the defeat by

Cumberland at Whitehaven, also in 1963. But his club career was not quite over. He still had another couple of seasons playing his top quality rugby league football.

The 1964-65 season was, as most clubs' seasons are after winning the Challenge Cup, full of high expectation. Although virtually working all hours in the business, Vince still had the passion to play for his home town team and, whenever he could, trained as hard as ever. He started the season in the first two matches, Keighley at home and a 17 points to 5 win, with Oldham the second game at the Watersheddings and a loss by 23 points to 2. Vince missed the next four and came back for the return Oldham fixture at home but again a similar score line saw the 'Roughyeds' win the game, 21–2. Vince played twelve matches on the trot, winning five and losing seven, missed the 2–all draw at home to Leigh and was back the week after for the next seven games. Wins over, Blackpool away, Whitehaven home, Halifax home and Salford away, a 15 points to 5 loss to Barrow at home and a 5–5 draw at Halifax brought the season up to the Challenge Cup first round and a home tie against the tough Workington Town.

In a mud bath, both sides had chances to win the game on the day but the conditions won it and the two teams fought out yet another draw, 2–2. Vince missed the replay at Derwent Park because of a knock and the Cumberland boys showed their mettle with a gritty performance in defence to hold out for a 2–0 win, and oh, so close in a typically hard cup-tie.

Vince played only two further games that season, against Swinton at Station Road and against Leigh at Hilton Park, both lost. In all Vince played in 25 games out of a possible 40 that season. All the time the business was taking more and more time. Various off-shoots of his family business concern included the welding shop, the scrap metal side, the pubs and hotels and the haulage company. The season as a whole was disappointing with the kick-on effect, by winning at Wembley the previous year, never materialising. Jim Measures was top try scorer again with 14 tries and the final results for 40 games read, played 40, won 16, lost 21, drawn 3.

Vince soldiered on into season 1965-66 and went into his fifth campaign for Widnes. Almost thirty-three and unlike many of his opponents for that number 13 jersey, he was still playing at loose forward. In an era of so many world class number 13s, Vince continued at last man down until he retired. The situation in that final season was that Vince played in 17 of the 42 club games and did play at loose man on 16 October 1965 against Huddersfield at Fartown the day after his 33rd birthday. As the cups went that season, Widnes went out of the Lancashire Cup in round one, at home to Warrington, by a very close, 12 points to 9. The 1965-66 season saw a new trophy introduced, the BBC Floodlit Trophy. This competition, as its name implied, was played under floodlights and began in October with the final usually played mid-December. The games were played mid-week and were popular amongst the supporters. Vince played in the first ever Floodlit Trophy game for Widnes against Warrington at Wilderspool and the result was a good win by 20 points to 10. Vince missed the second round win, 19–8, at home to Swinton and the 12 points to 9 defeat, at home, to the eventual winners, Castleford. The Challenge Cup started with an expected win, at home, over the amateur side from Wakefield, Brookside, who had recently changed their name from Wakefield Loco, by 23 points to 5. Round two saw the hard to beat Bradford Northern arrive at Naughton Park. The game was played on 19 March 1966 and the result was Widnes 6 Bradford Northern 7. It was Vince's final game as a professional player.

It was a sad end for Vince as he walked off the Naughton Park pitch. It would be the last time that the crowd roared at him with delight or anger, depending which side they were supporting, as the crunching tackle came in, or the skip through the defensive line and the perfectly timed pass would send a teammate over for a try. No more would the supporters gasp as Vince Karalius cleared his line with a bull-like run. No longer would opposing scum halves cringe as the shadow of the flying tackle covered them and wingmen had no need to fear the tough cover tackling Karalius any more.

But all the memories were stored away. The debut against Warrington when he was given the hardest of baptisms, the first Wembley trip as travelling reserve, the great Jim Sullivan, his selection for the Rest of the League against the Kiwi's at Bradford, his travels to play for Saints when serving the Queen in the army. Memories galore, of the Halifax Wembley win, the great Tom Vollenhoven and cheeky chappy Alex Murphy in the never to be forgotten Championship Final at Odsal against Hunslet, the Wembley win over the Rovers of Hull Kingston, his lasting friendships with the late hero Alan Prescott and his big mate, Dick Huddart. But above all, Vince's participation in the 1958 tour of Australia. That test match debut in Brisbane against all the odds, the second 'Rorkes Drift'.

Things happen in ones life that niggle when you hear them, for instance Vince gets fed up with the now seemingly permanent nickname, that every Englishman wishes was his, 'The Wild Bull of the Pampas'. It was given to Vince by his admiring enemies, it was Vince's own hard earned epithet, yet it belonged to all of us who adored his style of play. To the kid in the playground who called out to his mates, 'I'm Vince

Karalius, the Wild Bull'. To the man in the office who read of Vince's success on that tour and wished he was out in Australia with Vince instead of his office in Dewsbury. To the building workers in Manchester who cheered as they relayed the result via the radio of that great victory in Brisbane then the crushing win at the Cricket Ground in Sydney in that vital final test. Vince is his own man, a legend within the world's greatest and hardest team sport and if he hates the term then we should respect that, but, Vince made the legend and is the legend so therefore we should also be able to remember his deeds and the name his Aussie enemies feared, The Wild Bull of the Pampas.

One sometimes forgets the part wives and family members play in the careers of legends. Barbara has been a proud and wonderful supporter for Vince and the value of that support is immeasurable. In turn, Vince was the perfect role model for brothers Dennis and Anthony (Tony), who both became professional rugby league players and both played with Vince in club football, Dennis at Saints and Tony at Widnes. Tony Karalius played at Widnes, Saints and Fulham and indeed earned five Great Britain caps as a well respected hooker.

So the former Saint and Chemic loose forward had come to the end of a fifteen-year career as a player. The game and its participants had changed in that long and enjoyable period. He had seen great players retire, great coaches move on and even to the end, the excitement and glamour of the Rugby League Challenge Cup, not to mention the winning bonuses, had moved him to make that cup tie against Bradford Northern his swan song. Partnerships between players are fairly well established in the game of rugby league. Half-backs, or centres and wingmen make up most of them, Fleming and Helme (Warrington), Shannon and

McCue (Widnes), Williams and Jenkins (Leeds), Davies and Ward (Bradford), Mountford and Bradshaw (Wigan), Murphy and Smith (Saints), or Ashton and Boston (Wigan), Davies and Cracknell (Oldham), Devery and Cooper (Huddersfield) and Vollenhoven and Large (Saints). Partnerships also come, from what purists call the 'boiler-room', the back three, of the two second rowers and the loose forward, Foster, Tyler and Traill (Bradford), Clues, Watson and Owens (Leeds), Ryan, Bath, Palin (Warrington), Cherrington, Collier and Evans (Wigan), Silcock, Parsons and Karalius (Saints), Measures, Collier and Karalius (Widnes), Thompson, Edgar and Iveson (Workington Town).

Vince's four seasons at Widnes developed the Measures, Collier, Karalius partnership and it was whilst playing in a big match that Vince remembers big Frank Collier being presented, along with his teammates, before the game to His Royal Highness, The Duke of Edinburgh. As the Duke walked slowly down the line of players, shaking hands with each one and having a quick word, big Frank was at the end of the line and, being a typical Wigan lad, was never short of a few words himself. As the Duke offered his hand to Frank, the huge second rower said, in that thick Wigan brogue, 'Hello sir, how's the wife and kids?' whilst shaking the royal hand with gusto. Taken aback for a split second, the Duke recovered to smile at Frank and say, 'Fine, thank you and how are yours?' Great stuff before a big game!

Vince then left rugby league in 1966 and returned as a coach in 1972. In his time away from the game he concentrated on building the family business and actually found time to make a come-back in a one-off charity game for a player, Jack Pimblett, who was tragically killed in an amateur game for Pilkington Recs, when Salford took on an 'All Stars' team at the Willows. Brian Bevan turned out on the wing and amongst a plethora of former stars, Glyn Moses, Brian McGinn, Frank Myler and Vince were included. A great player and very nice man indeed was 'Bev', but just on rare occasions, he could be a bit grumpy, especially if he had bombed a try or someone hadn't given him the ball at the correct time. Anyway, Bevan romped over four times in this charity game and because Vince had always, more than not, played against Bev, and tried to rough it up a bit with him, he thought he would congratulate the great wingman on being so fit and still maintaining his electric pace. 'Well done Brian, another four tries, eh, you look in good nick' said Vince. The great Bev, forever the perfectionist, just looked at Vince and growled, 'I should have had seven', and walked away!

Vince also gained another interest at this time assisting with the training of one of Britain's top track athletes, Bill Hartley. Bill was a member of the successful 4 x 400 meters relay team that took the silver medal in the 1974 Commonwealth Games and gold in the European Games in Rome. Bill's wife, Donna, was herself a champion runner and took the Gold medal in the 1978 Commonwealth Games 400 metres, and also a Bronze medal in the 4 x 400 metres relay in the 1980 Moscow Olympics. Working on stride pattern and stamina training Vince would use his cine camera to take a film record of Bill as he flew around the track, then analysed the approach to the hurdles, take off and landing. Besides working with Bill and Donna Hartley, Vince also worked with the Liverpool sprinter and British Champion, Brian Green. He also ventured into after-dinner speaking and, because of his beliefs in weight training spoke to various sporting bodies on the subject of training for differing sports. Many years before today's modern training programmes, Vince was beating the drum, insisting that the game of rugby league required not only big, strong men to play it, but it needed big, strong athletes. He spoke at length of the need to introduce weights into the game's fitness programmes and actually was the man who brought this regime into both the Widnes and Wigan sides when employed as coach to those clubs. A little while later Vince was also responsible for the training of some rugby league players for a different game. The BBC introduced a new programme of immense interest when it brought on Superstars which involved athletes from various sports who competed in tests of strength, speed, stamina and awareness. Keith Fielding (Salford) and Des Drummond (Leigh) were possibly the two rugby league men remembered but Vince prepared Joe Lydon and Eric Hughes, both from his Widnes squad, to compete in the programme and they both won their heats.

7

COACHING AT THE TWO 'PARKS': NAUGHTON AND CENTRAL

In the close season 1971-72, the former tough centre/second rower, Don Gullick, resigned as coach at Widnes. The famous old club had drifted away from the hard to beat reputation it had revived under Vince's playing lead. It needed a shot in the arm. The club also needed someone in charge who identified with it, a local, a town hero, a personality. The Widnes chairman, Mr Frank Devonald, contacted Vince to see if he would be interested in coaching his home town team. Vince said that he would coach Widnes but totally on his terms. He must have complete control of all team affairs, of buying and selling, of team selection and most importantly, he must be kept informed of any major changes that impacted on the team. In the early 1970s this was tantamount to a takeover by the coach as most clubs at that time still held onto the ancient method of the board or committee selecting the team, or at least having a say in its format. Buying and selling players was a sore point in those days too as the players were classed solely as club assets, to be sold like so much meat on the hoof, therefore to allow the coach to have the say on whether or not a player stayed with, or left the club, was very much a new and delicate matter.

But a policy was agreed between Vince and the Widnes board and he was ensconced into the position of senior club first team coach.

The news of Vince's appointment hit the town of Widnes like a tidal wave. It set the place alight with the topic of rugby league football and in no time at all the town was buzzing with expectation. To say that the town and the club were hoping for a revival of good fortune is an understatement. Everyone knew Vince and his reputation around the town and remembered what he had brought to the table when he arrived as a player from St Helens some ten years before, he was the ideal man to follow Don Gullick.

With things going awry at the club his return was a masterstroke of timing as, if the wrong man had been appointed, it could well have exacerbated the difficulties at Naughton Park. The crowds had dwindled at an alarming rate due to the team's poor form but as Vince introduced his style of coaching to his squad of players, they responded instantly. His personality and his reputation of being a winner shone through and the players loved it. As one well-known authority on Widnes's club history put it, 'average players became good players and good players became great players almost overnight under the guidance of Vince Karalius'. Praise indeed.

Vince was shrewd enough to realise the potential of several young lads whom he inherited. He was also clever enough to wait to see if he could enlighten a few other players and make them good enough to win something big at the club before he asked the board for money to strengthen the squad. He, in fact, did what all coaches would like to do, that is give every one of the inherited players a fair chance to cement a first team place.

Vince was half way to being a great coach as his

motivational skills had been honed as a leading player in every side he represented. He had seen rugby league football at almost every level, from grass roots at West Bank, through A team rugby, into the first team and at the apex of the game, for Great Britain on an Ashes-winning tour. His own physical condition was a yardstick for others he was teaching to follow, as his charges knew the man and for what he stood – fitness, courage, determination and a winning habit. He moulded the youngsters in the squad into a tough, hard working body who went on after Vince to establish the Widnes club as a 'family' of rugby league players who honestly believed that they could lick the world! Almost all of the younger players went on either in coaching or playing to big things.

The main members of Vince's squad in his first season were Dutton, Brown, Prescott, Aspey, Gaydon, Hughes, Dennis O'Neill, Bowden, McLoughlin, Ashton, Warlow, Doughty, Nelson, Foran, Elwell, Walsh, Macko, Sheridan, Adams, Kirwan, Dearden, Nicholls, Reynalds and Blackwood. As the season progressed, the football played by the side improved, the defence became tougher, the team played to a definite pattern and the spectators began to return.

The first chance of cup glory came in the Lancashire Cup, played at the very start of the season. Two home wins against Blackpool Borough by 22 points to 4 and Rochdale Hornets by 17 points to 8 sent Widnes into the semi-final against Saints at Knowsley Road. It was a great occasion for Vince and he must have given a thought to his days under both Jim Sullivan and Alan Prescott when the Lancashire Cup was won on several occasions. This time it was Vince who came away the victor as his new team played wonderfully well to gain a nail-biting 12 points to 10 victory taking them into the final against Wigan. Reg Bowden and Dave Macko scored the tries and Ray Dutton kicked three goals.

The venue for the final was Knowsley Road and although Widnes played their hearts out the result was a win for Wigan by 15 points to 8, O'Neill and Gaydon scoring their tries and Mal Aspey kicking one goal. The Widnes side in the final was: Dutton; Brown, McLoughlin, Aspey, Gaydon; O'Neill, Bowden; Warlow, Foran, Doughty, Kirwan, Walsh and Nicholls. The Wigan side was more compact and the players for the Cherry and Whites were: Tyrer; Eastham, Francis, Fuller, Wright (Gandy); D Hill, Ayres; Ashcroft, Clarke, Fletcher, Ashurst, K O'Loughlin and Laughton.

Widnes's league programme was a little erratic, winning then losing alternately and only towards the season's end did the team gel and put together some consistent results gaining eleven victories out of the last thirteen games. But Vince was pleased with an earlier performance when the 1971 Kiwi tourists played at Widnes and in a thrilling game just pipped the local Widnes boys by 18 points to 15. There was also a cracking win over St Helens by 19 points to 9 which satisfied Vince immensely. Another great win in that first season was at Central Park against Wigan in the BBC Floodlit Trophy game by 15 points to 10 but a few weeks later the side went to lowly Huyton and could only manage a 2-all draw. Very frustrating for the coach.

The team finished in an acceptable eleventh position and qualified for the top sixteen play-offs. A good result at Swinton, with McLoughlin, O'Neill and Brown scoring tries and Dutton kicking three goals gave Vince a splendid 15 points to 11 win. The next play-off game was against Leeds at Headingley but in the top sixteen competition it was too big an ask for Widnes to beat the star-studded Leeds on the big, wide Headingley pitch and the season ended with a 20 points to 9 defeat

The Challenge Cup too had proved disappointing with the first of two trips to Headingley in knock-out competitions. A first round defeat by 17 points to 8 had seen another gutsy performance but unfortunately the two tries by O'Neill and Macko and Aspey's goal were not enough. A look at the ratio of wins in Vince's first season in coaching shows that after playing 34 games, Widnes won 19, lost 13 and drew 2. The major fact was that Vince's side had competed in their first spell together and that laid a strong foundation for later successes. The strong running former Royal Marine, Brown, was the top try scorer with 27 touchdowns and the ultra consistent Ray Dutton kicked 114 goals. After the good start in the County Cup, Widnes failed to consolidate their win at Wigan in the Floodlit Trophy as they went out against Rochdale Hornets, 6–5, away; and a 10–all draw at home to Wakefield Trinity in the John Player trophy led to a 12 points to 10 defeat at Belle Vue in the replay. The Challenge Cup dream had evaporated at Leeds but as the close season came around, Vince took the team's strengths and weaknesses into consideration after the first season and laid his plans to produce a consistent and cup winning side.

The 1972-73 season saw the Lancashire Cup being played as normal at the beginning of September. Already four league games had been played and Widnes had won three and lost one, at Wilderspool, Warrington, by 13 points to 4. The fifth game of the season was the County Cup first round at Hilton Park, Leigh. Vince knew from experience that this would be a hard one but he was delighted with his team when they registered a fine 20 points to 6 win. Mal Aspey led the way with a brace of tries, Nicholls and Prescott followed him over the line with one try each, Aspey landing four goals.

A very useful Dewsbury side were beaten at home, 21–7, then came the second round of the County Cup and St Helens. Vince relished this confrontation with his former club. Widnes was his club now but the magic of Saints in a big match still lit the fires under Vince. He selected from strength and sent out, Dutton; Prescott, O'Neill, Lowe, Aspey; Bowden, Ashton; Warlow, Elwell, Sheridan, Macko, Foran and Nicholls, to do battle. The result was a wonderful 13 points to 2 win, Lowe scoring a try with Dutton, 4, and Nicholls, 1, kicking goals. The team were performing very well, responding to Vince's tactics and patterns of play. Widnes suffered a reverse at Castleford when beaten 15–8 but rightened the ship with two big wins over Doncaster away in the Players No 6 Trophy and Rochdale Hornets at home in the league.

Swinton in the semi-final of the Lancashire Cup were the next opponents and the bonus was that Widnes were at home. Vince had to make changes because of injury and moved O'Neill from centre to stand-off to the exclusion of Bowden. Eric Hughes who missed the Saints win because of injury went into the centre for O'Neill and Blackwood in the second row for Macko. Swinton were a power in the league in those days and had a strong side who played some good football. They certainly did in this semi-final as they beat Widnes by 13 points to 4, Ray Dutton landing two consolation goals. The whole side were disappointed as the Saints win had made Widnes look so good in this competition.

Swinton took on star-studded Salford in the final and were beaten convincingly 25–11 at Warrington. Widnes couldn't afford to cry over spilt milk though as they were still in the Players No 6 and the lucrative Floodlit Trophy was looming in the near future. Around late October Vince captured one of the most confrontational forwards in the modern game when he signed big Jim Mills, the Welsh international prop who had come north to join Halifax when still only young and had just had a spell in Australia. Jim later toured Australia with the Lions twice, in 1974 and 1979.

The second round of the Players No 6 was a torrid affair against Warrington at Wilderspool. In a bruising, battling game the sides ended the 80 minutes at 18 points all. Brown, Aspey, Doherty and Elwell scored tries and Ashton, 2, and Aspey, 1, kicked goals. In the replay, another very close match gave Widnes the victory by 14 points to 11, with Brown, 2, Aspey and Hughes notching tries and Dutton adding 1 goal. Jim Mills made his debut in this game and was an immediate hit with the Widnes faithful. The third round had Widnes travelling to St Helens and the Saints were in no mood to fall again for Vince's tricks and tactics. This time Saints beat Widnes by 10–3 and another cup competition went out of the window.

The cups left for Widnes to win now were the Floodlit Trophy, the Challenge Cup and the Championship. The first on the agenda was the Floodlit Trophy and a top scalp was taken when the strong Leeds team came to Naughton Park. The Widnes defence was at its best as free scoring Leeds were beaten 9–4, Eric Hughes dashing in for a try and Ray Dutton kicking 3 goals. Batley fell next in a good Widnes home win by 21–8, then a great win over Wakefield Trinity at home by 16 points to 9 and they were into another final. Their opponents were the very fast and well organised Leigh and Widnes could find no way through their excellent defence. The Hilton Park men won a very tough and close run match by 5 points to nil.

The Challenge Cup draw brought Blackpool Borough to Naughton Park in round one and the class of the Widnes youngsters told as the 'Black and Whites' strolled to a 53 points to 3 victory. Round two saw Widnes make the short trip to Warrington but it was a defeat waiting for them as the 'Wire' produced a powerful display and took the game by a surprising 20 points to 8. In January 1973, Widnes sold the excellent George Nicholls to Saints. A local Widnes lad, George had been a cornerstone of Vince's pack. A powerful player who was best suited at loose forward but could play virtually anywhere in the pack, George went on to fill a similar role for Lancashire County and the Great Britain international side. Vince acted smartly and stepped in to bring the experienced Doug Laughton from Wigan. Laughton, the former Saints player before being transferred to Wigan, had been a member of the superb Lions tour of Australia and New Zealand that had won the ashes back in 1970, he also went on to captain the 1979 tour after missing out on the 1974 tour. Vince saw Laughton as the ideal man to guide his youngsters on the field. With the additional earlier signing of Jim Mills, Vince now had the makings of a big strong pack, with both youth and experience in it. But one must also realise just how much an impression Vince made on the up-and-coming youngsters at Naughton Park. Older players too, players who may have thought that they would retire without winning a major trophy, suddenly found that they were in with a chance in whichever cup the club were competing in.

Vince had only been back at the club two seasons and from being 'down in the dumps' they were showing what a force they would be in just a few short seasons time. Players who prospered with Vince as coach – Elwell, O'Neill, Nicholls, Aspey, McLoughlin, George, Hughes, Sheridan, Adams, Foran and Macko – all did extremely well in the game and the accepted best uncapped half-back in the game,

Reg Bowden, was handled superbly by Vince. His association with his home town team paved the way for an almost unmatchable extended run, not only in cup football but in the everyday league matches too, until the emergence of the great Wigan side of the late 1980s and 1990s. The dynasty Vince created earned the proud title of 'The Cup Kings', and the ground at the then Naughton Park, was the graveyard of teams visiting there.

So the 1972-73 season ended with Widnes finishing in twelfth place and earning the right to visit Wakefield Trinity in the play-offs. The Trinity team, always good at Belle Vue, relished the advantage of this home tie and playing some exhilarating football early on, took a lead that they increased as the game progressed and at the final whistle won through 33 points to 6.

While the season had not been a breathtaking success, neither had it been a failure. But it had served as a holding period while that bunch of young, hungry players started to achieve their potential. Mal Aspey had 24 tries as top try scorer, with Eric Hughes and Dennis O'Neill 20 tries apiece, Ray Dutton obliged with 71 goals and Aspey kicked 50. They were almost there, ready to grasp their opportunity to become a real force amongst the big clubs.

Vince's third season as Widnes coach coincided with the club's centenary. The old Lancashire Cup came around again and a first round tie against Salford at the Willows saw another disappointment with a 12 points to 11 defeat. Dewsbury were then taken on in the Players No.6 Trophy but the visit to Crown Flatts again ended in a 35–24 defeat. The problem was that for the first half of the season Vince hardly had the same team available for two games on the trot as he was forced, through injuries, to swap and change. The 1973 touring Aussies came to Naughton Park and won 25–10 but early in October the Floodlit Trophy draw sent Widnes away yet again in knock-out football. They had to travel to their old antagonists Leigh and recorded a good win 13–10. Now this was the dreadful period of strikes and the three day working week. The electricity supplies were threatened and power cuts became a regular occurrence across the country, so to save the Floodlit Trophy, all matches were played mid-week in the afternoons.

Following the Floodlit game at Leigh, Widnes played six games, five were lost and one was a 15 points all draw at Castleford so by the time the next round against Salford came along, confidence was not particularly high in the Widnes ranks. However the match was at home and a hard fought winning way was found giving Widnes victory by 15 points to 11.

Bramley were slugged at home in the league 27–6 and this was followed by the semi-final of the Floodlit Trophy competition. Hull Kingston Rovers were the tough opponents and the match was at Craven Park, Hull. In a superb contest Widnes pulled out all the stops to charge into the BBC Floodlit Trophy final 13–8. Brown zoomed in for a try and Dutton kicked 4 goals and Elwell 1. In the meantime, little Bramley were breaking all their old club's records by fighting their way through, against all the odds, to be the other finalists.

It was a triumph for Bramley just to be there as in almost 80 years of existence the club had never reached a final of any description before. Their player/coach was the excellent former Great Britain and Hull FC Full-back, Arthur Keegan, who had some handy players under his tuition but not in any way as good as Vince had in the Widnes squad. The final was played at Naughton Park and one of the biggest upsets in the game's history occurred when the little Davids of the village of Bramley, who had, since day one of their existence, been in the very big shadows of both Hunslet and Leeds, beat the Goliaths of Widnes by 15 points to 7. Everyone in the game thought it a misprint in the newspapers but it was a fact, on the day it was big Bramley for once in their long and unsuccessful history. The Widnes side that suffered the shock defeat was: Dutton; O'Neill, Hughes, Aspey, Macko; Warburton, Bowden; Hogan, Elwell, Nelson, Sheridan, Blackwood and Laughton. Macko scored the Widnes try and Dutton two goals. No one ever found out what Vince said to his players at half time, or at full time, but many in the game wished to have been a fly on the dressing room wall!

The run up to the Challenge Cup was still hit and miss but a cracking win at home over Wakefield Trinity in round one, by 27 points to 7 held out a promise of bigger things. The second round had Widnes travelling the short yet, unsuccessful journey, to Leigh where an 11 points to 7 result had them bid farewell to Wembley once again. This defeat was harder to take as only the week before Widnes had gained a good 17 points to 10 win over Leigh at Naughton Park.

People say that rugby league football is a funny old game, ask Vince and he will agree. After the cup defeat at Hilton Park against Bramley, Widnes played 13 games and won 12 of them, including two super doubles over Wigan and Saints. The late run of successive wins took Widnes up the league ladder to finish in fourth place and a brave attempt at winning the Championship ended at Leeds when the Yorkshire team won a very close game by 20 points to 15. The side played a total of 42 games: 23 were won, 18 lost and 1 drawn. Prescott was the leading try scorer with 14 and Dutton again went passed the century with 129 goals.

The reasons for describing the statistics of the various cup ties and key league games is to review the progress of Vince's career in coaching. Being a playing legend does not always guarantee that person success in the coaching sphere. Playing and coaching are like chalk and cheese and if a great player can attain the same level in coaching then he can be called a natural. Vince made the transition almost immediately and with the success that proves his coaching expertise, as said earlier, he made ordinary players into good ones and good players into great ones. Results are vital, and Vince certainly improved the Widnes results. Good team spirit is paramount to any successful side, Vince improved team spirit. Players and tactics must be checked and bettered, Vince made almost all the squad better players and introduced good, workable tactics. His overall success, that was prepared and worked for over three seasons, was achieved, in spades, during his fourth and final season as senior coach at the club

The first league game of the 1974-75 season should have been Dewsbury at Naughton Park. I was the coach at Dewsbury at that time and the players were up in arms about pay! Mick 'Stevo' Stephenson had just left the club and moved, lock, stock and barrel, family and all, to Penrith in Australia. The players were asked to take a cut in pay and came out on strike. The refusal to play went throughout the club and A team players also came out in sympathy with their first team mates. The strike lasted for three weeks and was only resolved when the club committee – Dewsbury was a members club at that time – revised their thinking and offered the previous season's terms plus a bit! One of the casualties was the game at Widnes. Instead of taking on the Dewsbury club as a good warm up first game, the 'Chemics' went into the cauldron of Wilderspool to take on the tough, no-nonsense Warrington.

In another bruising battle Widnes fought their way to a very creditable 8–all draw. With Aspey and Prescott scoring tries and Dutton one goal. Vince realised that this could well be a good season if the players could regain that essential self-belief that had just left them temporarily. And he reasoned the best way was to lift the tempo of their hard training routines even higher. When it came to the Warrington game the fitness of the Widnes lads was there to see and the superb physical condition of the team certainly contributed to the winning of this vital league point. But no respite as the next game was a first round Lancashire Cup tie at the dreaded Watersheddings to face Oldham. Fitness told again as a good win was forged on the backs of the Widnes pack. Playing perfect cup-tie football the forwards took control of the game and Dutton's trusty boot landed four precious goals to go with two fine tries from Hughes and Bob Blackwood, to give a 14 points to 9 win. Another good win came in the league game at Belle Vue, Wakefield 12 points to 6 but then came two gruelling, hard-fought cup ties against Rochdale Hornets. The first one, at the Athletic Ground, was a dour 7 all draw, with three Dutton goals and a Keith Elwell drop goal. The replay, three days later, was another hard, tight game with Widnes just easing through by 8 points to 7, with tries by Mick George and Eric Hughes and one goal from Ray Dutton. The hard road in the Lancashire Cup continued with the ultra tough tie, Leigh away. But Vince now had this team ticking and it was little surprise when Widnes marched through to the final with a wonderful 8–5 win. Mick Adams scored two tries and Ray Dutton one goal in this cracking victory. As in the previous season, the Widnes side put together a fine winning sequence, and in the first fourteen cup and league games, they lost only one and drew two, one of those being the cup tie at Rochdale.

Reaching the County Cup final in 1974-75 had also given Vince a remarkable record after taking over an ailing club. He had guided Widnes to a final in each of his four seasons. In 1971-72 it was the Lancashire Cup final v Wigan, in 1972-73 it was the BBC Floodlit Trophy final v Leigh, in 1973-74 Widnes were involved against Bramley in the Floodlit Trophy again and now, in 1974-75 they were once more in the Lancashire Cup, against the speedy Salford, at Wigan. But the three runners up medals did not suit Vince. He wanted winner's medals and cups to fill the cupboard at his club. This game against Salford offered a genuine chance of winning one of the big cups in the game.

Vince had skippered the 1964 Widnes side that last picked up the Challenge Cup. Before that it had been 1937 when the cup was lifted by the club. The Lancashire Cup had last been won by Widnes in 1945 so it was high time it came back to Naughton Park. However, a meagre crowd of 7,403 turned out to watch his important, traditional cup final as Widnes paraded their battling side, one which had won by 5 points away at Oldham, a draw and replay win by one point against Rochdale and a nail-biter at Leigh by three points, all the games had been a struggle and they had come through. Against Salford, Vince knew the danger would come from Paul Charlton, the fast attacking full-back, Keith Fielding and Maurice Richards, the two flying ex-rugby union international wingmen, both with pace to burn. Also Knighton, Coulman and Eric Prescott were fast, powerful running forwards who would take some watching.

The two teams lined up thus: Widnes: Dutton; George, O'Neill, Aspey, Prescott; Hughes, Bowden; Mills, Elwell, Stephens, Adams, Blackwood and Laughton. Salford: Charlton; Fielding, Dixon, Graham, Richards; Taylor,

Banner; Mackay, Devlin, Grice, Knighton, Coulman and E. Prescott.

Fred Lindop from Wakefield was the man with the whistle and it turned out to be a game just as hard and unrelenting as any of the previous ties.

The game swayed firstly one way, then the other but all Salford had to show was a Keith Fielding penalty goal. Widnes on the other hand were a determined lot and the hard running Mick George crashed over for a good try then a Ray Dutton goal and a neat drop goal by Eric Hughes brought the majestic old Lancashire Cup home to Widnes with a score of Widnes 6 Salford 2. Salford's Mike Coulman was deemed to have been the best player of the match and won the 'Rugby Leaguer' award.

It was sweet music to Vince's ears as the lads celebrated in the Central Park dressing room. His first cup as coach and winning it with a team he had brought back to life. Another couple of league wins on the trot followed the cup victory before the club were brought down to earth with a bang as the first round of one of their favourite cup competitions took them to the old Greyhound Stadium in Leeds to take on the re-formed former Hunslet side now called New Hunslet in the Floodlit Trophy. Filled with cheap signings and older players and playing on a postage stamp sized ground, these re-formed A teamers and 'has beens' caught Widnes on a glue pot of a pitch and, playing their hearts out, beat the strong Widnes side by 12 points to 5. Welcome to the lower reaches boys!

Vince and most of his team had tasted this humble pie before in the Floodlit Trophy when another Leeds side, Bramley, had come to Naughton Park and walloped Widnes in the final only the season before, so they knew how to fix the wheels back on quickly. One thing that certainly helped

Vince in his efforts to get back to winning ways was that in October 1974 the club signed a top Australian back, Chris Anderson, who returned later with the 1978 and 1982 Kangaroos. Anderson's home town club was the Catholic orientated Canterbury Bankstown and Chris was a huge success at Widnes. Heaven knows what he thought when he turned out at New Hunslet, on that ultra small ground, its 'tuning fork' grid-iron style posts and all that good old Yorkshire mud, coming, as he had, from the sun-drenched, modern stadiums of Sydney!

Winning more league games than they were losing, Widnes's next objective was the No. 6 Trophy. Wakefield Trinity was an early faller before the onslaught and were crushed at Naughton Park by 35 points to 13. Swinton at home were the next and the Station Road team, so often the Widnes nemesis were beaten 15–5. A titanic struggle ensued in the semi-final round as the strong Hull Kingston Rovers outfit fought like tigers but to their credit, Widnes showed the grit and determination that Vince was preaching. A close run win by 16 points to 14 put the Chemics into the final to play Bradford Northern who had beaten Whitehaven in the other semi-final.

The final was played at Warrington and again only 5,935 watched the game, played on a quagmire of a pitch, as the balding, yet still young, Stuart Carlton slid over by the corner flag, in the mud, for the only try of the weather-spoilt final, Ray Dutton had kicked one consolation goal for Widnes. Another final for Vince's coaching but another runners up medal. The teams in that mud bath were: Widnes: Dutton; Prescott, O'Neill, Aspey, Anderson; Hughes, Bowden; Mills. Elwell, Sheridan, Adams, Blackwood and Laughton. Bradford Northern: Carlton; Francis, Ward, Gant, D, Redfearn, Blacker, Seabourne; Earl, Jarvis, Jackson, Joyce,

Trotter and Fearnley.

The League trundled on and a surprise packet were Featherstone Rovers who finished one above Widnes in fourth place, with Leeds third, Wigan second and Saints at the top of the ladder. Featherstone Rovers did the double over Widnes as did Saints but both Wigan and Leeds were beaten by Widnes in league football. Following the previous season's fourth place to finish a close fifth at least showed the consistency that Vince was looking for. After this decent position in the league and the Lancashire Cup in the cupboard, plus the John Player final, all that was needed now to make a world beating season was a good run in the Challenge cup. Around it came again, the beautiful old cup that has retained so many wonderful memories and also so many sorrowful ones.

The old enemy Swinton at Station Road was the first venue. Many a good side had left their ambitions on that king-sized playing area but Widnes went in the right frame of mind and with the right team. In another tight one Widnes slid home by 13 points to 4 and Anderson, Elwell and Peek, a back rower with only a handful of first team games, scored the tries and the ever reliable Ray Dutton kicked with his usual accuracy to land two goals. One down, four to go, as the draw read, Hull FC will play Widnes! Oh no, another tough away trip, where are all the home draws?

Although not quite the daunting draw it was in Vince's playing days, it was still bad enough. Vince worked the team well in preparation for a hard fixture. The day dawned and what a game! In a typical, old fashioned, brutal cup tie, Widnes and Hull slugged it out and at the whistle it was Hull 12 Widnes 13. The try heroes were Aspey and George with Dutton landing three goals and Mick Adams a vital drop goal. Again, everyone was around the telly as the draw was made – Oldham will play Widnes! Swinton, Hull and now Oldham, if they got to Wembley they would not have played one of the five rounds at home, as the semi-final, and of course the final, are played on neutral grounds.

One thing that should be said, is that whilst both Hull and Oldham were in the second division at this time, they were still terrible places to go in a cup tie. The Watersheddings crowd were waiting for Widnes and as usual it was very confrontational. In the old ground the spectators used to be very near the touchlines and the atmosphere was awesome.

Vince selected a couple of unfamiliar faces in his team, Mick George was in the centre, Terence 'Tucker' Karalius, a nephew of Vince, was on the wing and J Wood in the second row with Adams. Alan Ashton was on substitute duty.

Another outstanding all-round performance gained a notable win for the 'Black and Whites' with an Adams try, three Dutton goals and an Ashton drop goal adding up to the 10 points that Widnes scored to Oldham's 4 and Vince was one more step nearer his Wembley dream once again.

In the Widnes centenary season, only one year before this great cup run, Vince was asked to pen a piece in honour of the event. I quote from the piece he wrote. 'I was born in Widnes, I am a Widnes lad. Although my career started down the road in St Helens. My greatest achievement, in my eyes, was leading Widnes to victory in the 1964 cup final. Some players come back home at the end of their careers and it's like putting a horse out to grass. Not for me that nonsense. I came back home determined to give the Widnes club 100% effort and I think I did that in that Wembley season. When we won the cup I was the proudest man on earth. As for the future, I would like to see Widnes have an outstanding team, like the old Wigan, with a beautiful ground to match the team, like Headingley, Central Park or the new complex at Salford. Widnes is a rugby Town with a population that loves its rugby. The spectators deserve success and I would like to play a part in giving it to them.'

Those words were said many years ago and reading them now, one realises how near Vince took the club to his dream. The team Vince built went on to be as good if not better than most teams in the Rugby Football League, they became 'the Cup Kings'. The club did get a state of the art ground and they did get into Super League and hold their own for a spell. The business of giving 100% went without saying so really Vince's dream came true in every aspect and due to the foundation work done by Vince and one or two more. But it's back to 1975 and Vince's men were to play Wakefield Trinity at Odsal, Bradford. Warrington would play Leeds in the other semi-final at Wigan. The halcyon days of huge crowds were over. Going back only a dozen years a crowd of well over 43,000 had watched Wakefield Trinity play Featherstone Rovers, neither club being particularly well supported but this semi-final, Widnes v Wakefield Trinity, drew only 9,155 people.

Trinity were around mid-table of a sixteen team first division and were still a handy unit. The Widnes team read: Dutton; Karalius, George, Aspey, Prescott; Hughes, Bowden; Mills, Elwell, Sheridan, Adams, Foran and Laughton. Vince raised one or two eyebrows around town with the selection of his nephew 'Tucker' Karalius but being around the houses once or twice he realised that should the team slip up in this big game, then the blame would be his and the question of his nephew foolishly raised. Vince selected the best team he thought on the day, the result would justify his selection or condemn him for nepotism. The tries by Laughton and Foran, plus three goals and a drop goal by Dutton did justify his selection as Wakefield were beaten by 13 points to 7

Over the next three weeks Widnes were sunk by Dewsbury, 31–7 at Crown Flatts, and 42–3 at Post Office Road, Featherstone. In between and after they beat Rochdale Hornets at home, 13–7 and Bradford Northern at home, 12–7. The final league game of the season was Leeds at home and as the 'Loiners' had soundly thumped them at Headingley, the Widnes team were hell bent on vengeance. Playing with the buoyancy of Wembley finalists and on an end of season sunny day, Widnes took Leeds to the cleaners with a scintillating display of fast, open rugby that had the crowd in raptures. Jenkins 3, Aspey and Dutton romped over for tries and Dutton landed three goals to give a decisive 21 points to nil to the 'Chemics' and wipe out that defeat at Headingley.

Salford came to Naughton Park in the play-offs and produced some entertaining football with their speedy backs and won 20 points to 12 but Widnes had their minds set on 10 May, Wembley day and the determination laid down by Vince was quickly kicking in. Peter Geraghty of York was the referee on the big day. Peter had come through the ranks, junior football, open age football, A team refereeing and finally first team football, and, the magical day at Wembley.

The scene was set. Two teams, only a stone's throw apart geographically, a derby match, Vince coaching Widnes and his old mate Alex Murphy coaching Warrington, a real Boy's Own story. 85,098 people attended the Final and saw a hard fought game with defences well on top. Each side scored one try, Jim Mills crashing in for Widnes and John Bevan crossing for Warrington. The game was decided by the sure boot of Mr Reliable, Ray Dutton, who once again proved invaluable to Widnes with his radar guided goal kicking. Ray kicked five goals and one neat drop goal.

Jim Mills' try and Dutton's goals gave Widnes 14 points whilst Bevan's try added to Derek Whitehead's two goals gave Warrington 7 points. Vince had done it again. His team had travelled the hard road and come up trumps. Ray Dutton deservedly picked up the coveted Lance Todd Trophy for the man of the match. The teams lined up thus: Widnes: Dutton; Prescott, George, Aspey, Anderson; Hughes, Bowden; Mills, Elwell, Sheridan, Adams, Foran and Laughton. Subs: T. Karalius, Nelson. The Warrington team was: Whitehead; M Philbin, Noonan, Reynolds, Bevan; Whittle, Gordon; Chisnall, Ashcroft, Wanbon, Conroy, Martyn and B. Philbin. Subs: Briggs, Nicholas.

A typical Widnes reception greeted coach Karalius, captain Doug Laughton and the team on arrival back at Naughton Park with the superb old cup. Vince had achieved the great milestone and huge honour only reached by a certain few. He had won the Rugby League Challenge Cup as a player, a captain and a coach. And at Wembley, that May afternoon, as that wonderful cup was brought down to the pitch from the Royal Box by Doug Laughton, two people were chaired around the field, Laughton and Vince. A super moment to remember forever!

But the old adage that you can't please all of the people all the time was well founded as despite all the honours and winning merits that Vince brought back to Widnes there were a few who found fault. In the selection of his nephew as substitute in the Wembley Final Vince earned the wrath of a few people who thought that Dennis O'Neill should have worn the number 14 jersey. The speedy utility back was an international player in his own right and he had played in 27 games during the Wembley season. But that was a little bit of sentiment and sentiment does not exist in the tough game of rugby league football, especially from a coach's point of view.

As in the earlier rounds, Vince selected his team on merit and, once again, he was found to be right. The side he chose were victorious.

Some sportsmen time their departure from their chosen sport to perfection. 'Go out at the top' some people say, others hang around for one fight or game too many. When the chairman had asked him to coach Widnes, Vince had told him, not only that he wanted full control but that his appointment would be for a limited period. Vince did not want the coaching job for the remainder of his life, he wanted to lift Widnes back up amongst the top echelon, ensure a good playing squad with good youngsters coming through and leave the club safe and sound. After the Wembley success he stood down as coach and despite the players coming en masse to ask him to reconsider, he stuck to his guns, he wanted to devote more time to his family and business interests. What could the club say? He had done all that he wanted for the club plus much more and the board of directors sadly accepted his resignation. A presentation was made to Vince of a silver salver, signed by the entire club, players, staff and board and a gold watch in grateful thanks for his superb service to Widnes RLFC. So ended another page in the Vince Karalius-Widnes RLFC book. It would not be opened again for another six years.

8

WIGAN, THE ISLE OF MAN, AND WIDNES, AGAIN

In September 1976, Joe Coan the Wigan coach resigned and left the club. Jack Hilton, the Wigan Chairman and former international wingman, called on Vince to ask him if he would be interested in coaching at Central Park. Vince had had a year out of the game and was feeling the old sensation of getting stuck in again and at a club with the kudos of Wigan who could blame him? In the season Vince had off, Wigan had finished fifth in the league table. But by the time Vince arrived at Central Park, the club were out of the Lancashire Cup. They had knocked out Saints in round one by 37 points to 5 but had lost, unexpectedly, to Leigh at Central Park 16–14 and this result may well have hastened Joe Coan's departure.

Vince's arrival coincided with a win over Salford at home, a good 13–all draw up in Workington, a cracking win in the Floodlit Trophy competition over his former charges, Widnes, a massive 33 points to nil victory in the John Player trophy against Keighley at home and another belting win at Central Park against Leeds by 10 points to 8 in the league. Looking back at the results before Vince joined the club, in the two games in August and the four in September only two were won. From the start of October five games were played and Vince's coaching produced four wins and a draw.

Now Vince's memory for names was not the best and one tale that came from his early Wigan days was when Tom Rathbone of the family of Rathbone's Bakers joined the Wigan board. The whole squad of players were invited to Tom's privately owned golf club, Holland Hall, the swish establishment on the outskirts of Wigan, for an introductory meal and to meet the new board member, Tom Rathbone. Jack Hilton asked Vince if he would say a few words of welcome to Tom and he agreed to do so. Now, as mentioned, Vince and names sometimes don't mix and whilst he started well enough in his welcome of Tom when it came to thanking him for his hospitality in having the full squad over for dinner, his thanks went something like this – or so I was led to believe. 'This evening has been so nice and also such a pleasure in meeting the new board member that I must thank Mr Warburton for his hospitality.' Right speech, unfortunately, wrong bakery! No one laughed louder than Tom Rathbone and the correct chord was struck.

York away at Clarence Street saw a loss in the John Player and two weeks later a defeat by 12 points to 5 at Leigh left behind the Floodlit Trophy. But league results picked up nicely and one or two brought a smile to Vince's face. Saints were beaten 14-12 at Knowsley Road over Christmas, Oldham and Featherstone Rovers were bested at home and a very good draw at Headingley, 13 all in mid January set the club up nicely for a good Challenge Cup run. It's funny how things work out, the first round draw took an amateur side, Pilkington Recs from, yes, St Helens to Central Park. The amateur lads did themselves proud with a fighting display that held the score to 10–4 at full time to Wigan. Then in the league, Widnes won 10–7 at Naughton Park. A grand 15–10 home win over Wakefield Trinity maintained Wigan's hold on a play-off place. But they might have known it, Saints away, were drawn in round two of the big cup and although losing, Wigan went out fighting with Saints going through 9–4, George Fairbairn kicking two goals. At the time it seemed that Vince could not get away from Saints or Widnes

A superb league double over Leigh, 27–9 at home and a thumping 40 points to nil at Hilton Park, plus a double over Barrow did their play-off chances no harm at all and a good home victory against Bradford Northern, 19–15, gave Vince a great March but April was not kind to the cherry and whites as an 8 points to 4 win over Rochdale Hornets at the Athletic Ground was scant reward for some good performances. The play-offs took Vince and his team to Knowsley Road and a good show there gave them a 10–10 draw. The replay at Wigan was hard fought but Saints went through in the end by 8 points to Wigan's 3. Vince's first season at Central Park ended with the team in seventh place.

In the close season Vince gradually brought weight training into the Central Park fitness routines. This was to pay dividends in the near future as Vince went into his first close season contemplating the stats of 15 league games won from 30 played, with 2 draws and 13 losses.

It was in this season just ended that Vince, only once, showed his tough, hard character to the Wigan squad. When I joined Wigan as coach in 1981-82 quite a few of the players had overlapped from Vince's recent era and there were tales galore abut him, not one of them bad, still being told in the Wigan dressing room. This story went thus: Leeds were drawn in the first round of the John Player Trophy at Headingley and a terrific win was achieved by 25 points to 22, Green Vigo scoring a memorable hat-trick of tries. When the draw for the second round was made, Wigan drew New

Hunslet, who had come up into the first division after gaining promotion from fourth place the season before. The Wigan directors decided that unlike the previous season, when Wigan drew Pilkington Recs and paid a big bonus for beating an amateur team, they would pay normal 'league' wages for a win against this South Leeds side, who should be beaten anyway, without a bonus for doing so but a big bonus would be paid in round three. The players were not amused as they had earned a great wage of £70 per man against Leeds in round one. Now they were told that they were on £35 per man to win in the second round. This was unacceptable to them. I suppose for goodwill, as the team were getting first division money for playing what had been a second division team, the players should have buckled down to winning the game, then asked for a good bonus for winning the following round against whoever it was. But when the Wigan players were told there would be no bonus for the second round of a cup competition, they were most upset. The way they saw it was that they had received a good bonus for beating Leeds in round one but how could the board pay them less for a win in round two, no matter who the opponents were. Talks of strike action arose and a militant group of players tried to gain the support of the A team not to play in the game should the board demand them to.

Now Vince would normally have steered clear of this trouble but he realised the stupidity of being knocked out of the John Player Trophy for failing to fulfil a cup fixture. He called a meeting in the dressing room and met the players to attempt to talk some common sense to them and get them to withdraw their threat. Vince spoke like a father to them, in gentle terms and pointing out the sensible way to act but the players said 'no'. Several times Vince tried to get through to them and almost succeeded but for about five militant players. With time running out Vince and the club knew that the Rugby Football League would come down heavily on Wigan should they not play New Hunslet and when Vince conducted a final meeting with them things got a bit heated and on his way out of the dressing room, Vince heard one of the players make a derogatory statement about Widnes people. That was it, not only would they not see sense, they tried a snide comment about his birthplace, Vince about turned back into the centre of the dressing room, 'What was that?' he growled. The Wigan players realised too late that they had made a big mistake. As is the norm, the culprit stayed quiet, but Vince was on the war path. 'I'm going outside into the passage. I want the coward who said that about Widnes to follow me and come outside. My parents are from Widnes, my brothers, sister and all my family are from Widnes, now get yourself outside the one that said it' and with that Vince strode out into the passage and slammed the door.

The players realised they had gone too far with this legend. Various players said, simultaneously, 'I never said anything' as they all sat rooted to the seats. The door flew open and in came Vince, 'I'm sorry lads, when I offered out the one who slagged Widnes, I was wrong, I overrated you, so any THREE of you Wiganers outside now!' Seeing this side of Vince brought them back down to earth but Jimmy Hornby helped diffuse the situation a bit when he said, 'Vince meant what he said about any of you Wiganers but I'm safe, I'm from Billinge!' (which is down the road from Wigan).

New Hunslet were beaten, 9 points to 7, but trouble was around the corner as the third round tie was played only two weeks later and money problems were raised again when the board offered £70 as winning money against Widnes away. A good half of the team went on a one-off boycott of the game, forcing Vince to play eleven A teamers out of the Fifteen places in the side. Needless to say Widnes won by 25 points to nil. Several key players missed the game and this knocked the team spirit that Vince had built. But the 1977-78 season had started much better for Vince and his men. The Lancashire Cup, now in a regular spot to start the season, was here again and what a start it was. The first two rounds were at Central Park and were, in fact, the first two games of the season.

Oldham came first and were swamped by 42 points 5, then, a week later, Whitehaven were treated no better when they were slaughtered 52–8. Just what Vince needed and the weights programme that he had introduced was taking effect. A journey to Fartown in the third week of the new season in the Floodlit Trophy gained Wigan their third win in three games as the Cherry and Whites won a hard one 22–18. The league began the following weekend and a daunting trip to Derwent Park to tackle those big Cumbrian lads up at Workington. The result delighted Vince and gave his boys an unblemished played four, won four as Wigan showed commitment in a 19–16 win and the team spirit seemed to be returning. This new-found commitment continued as Wakefield Trinity were beaten at Central Park by 19 points to 2.

After the first six games, six wins on the trot was a great start to any club's season. But Vince was a realist and knew that this great start had to end some time and with the County Cup semi-final against Warrington looming up Vince could excuse a defeat in the league but not in the one-off cup tie. The first defeat came the following weekend at the graveyard of Lancashire clubs, Post Office Road, Featherstone. The Rovers knew how to operate on that tight field and held off the Wigan thrust with a grand 19 points to 8 win. Next game was a big one all around, Warrington in the County Cup semi-final at Central Park. Playing like a Vince Karalius team, the Wigan side tackled bravely and tries by Vigo 2, Davies, Irving and Taylor and a goal by Nulty gave the home side the score of 17 points to Warrington's 8.

In the run to the County Cup Final, out of thirteen games played only three were lost, one of those three was the second round Floodlit Trophy game at Hull Kingston Rovers where Wigan went down by 18 points to 7. Leeds were beaten twice in that thirteen game run, once in the league at home by 27–15 and once away in the John Player Trophy first round, 25–22. Besides the losses at Featherstone and Hull Kingston Rovers, the third upset was at Odsal where Bradford Northern won 18–13. So the Lancashire Cup Final arrived on 29 October 1977. The venue was Wilderspool, Warrington and the opponents, Workington Town. A very close game ended with a Cumbrian victory by three points only at 16–13.

Vince selected Swann; Vigo, Davies, Willicombe, Hornby; Taylor, Nulty; Hogan, Aspinall, Irving, Ashhurst, Blackwood and Melling, Subs: Burke, Regan. Workington Town had on duty that day, Charlton; Collister, Risman, Wright, McCorquodale; Wilkins, Walker; Watts, Banks, Bowman, L Gorley, Pattinson and P Gorley. One sub used: Atkinson. The gate was 9,458. Wright and Wilkins scored tries for Town, McCorquodale kicked 4 goals and Walker dropped 2 goals. Wigan's scorers were Willicombe, Nulty and Ashurst with tries, Nulty and Burke kicked 1 goal each.

Disappointing to get a runners-up medal though it was, Wigan were back on the right road with a win over New Hunslet the following Wednesday evening at Central Park in the already mentioned John Player game by 9 points to 7. The loss to Workington Town had a delayed shock effect on Vince's team as after the New Hunslet scrape through, Wigan were beaten by Widnes, away in the third round John Player, 25–0, and consecutively by Warrington, home, 24–9, New Hunslet, home, 9–7, Hull, away, 13–0 and Leeds, away, 34–10. Vince got the team back on winning ways with a good 31–10 result at home over Hull and a battling 8 points to 5 victory over the strong Dewsbury side at Crown Flatts. But Saints caught them cold over Christmas at Central Park when they dished out a good hiding with a 24–13 win.

At this time at Wigan, Vince had a super back-up team of staff with two stalwarts of the game in Billy Wilkinson and the old war-horse, Peter Smethurst. Billy was used as a scout for the club, bringing many good young kids to Central Park and Peter, the greatest enthusiast for the game that ever was involved in it, was assistant coach to Vince. Wigan won four of the next five games as, besides a Lancashire Cup Final, they were going well in the first division that was being headed by three strong clubs, Hull Kingston Rovers, Warrington and Widnes. The Challenge Cup threw up another amateur team for Wigan in round one. The tough Leeds and District Champions, Dewsbury Celtic, one of the most consistent teams in the county, had won their way through, yet again, to the first round proper and their prize was a 'home' draw against Vince's side. Now Dewsbury Celtic were player/coached by an old player of mine from Bramley, and he joined me later at Halifax, the former Halifax prop forward, Terry Dewhirst. The game was played at the home of Batley RLFC, Mount Pleasant. The Celtic had plenty of former professional experience in their team and gave Wigan a real run for their money, but Hornby, Aspinall and Steve O'Neill scored tries and Fairbairn landed three goals to give a score of 15–5 to Wigan. Then the chance of another Wembley visit vanished when Bradford Northern visited Central Park and won in the second round in good style, 22–10.

The old enemy, Saints were beaten 22–17 at Knowsley Road in a particularly pleasing result for Vince and an exciting game with Hull Kingston Rovers at Wigan ended in a 23–all draw and in a cracking last fling of action four of the final five league games were won, taking Wigan into a very creditable fifth place in the table.

In the top eight play-off, Widnes were at home to Leeds, and it was Bradford Northern v Featherstone Rovers, Saints v Salford and Hull Kingston Rovers hosted Wigan at Craven Park. It was a bad day for Wigan as the fluent football of the 'Robins' ended Wigan's season with a strong 17–0 win.

In an effort to gain more size and power in his pack. Vince signed a giant of a lad for the number 8 position. Competitive scrimmaging was still in play then and it was imperative that any team had at least its share of the ball from the set scrum. Steve Breheny was the player and he was a big, strong lad. He was also a tough lad who knew his way around a street fight. His reputation preceded him as being a handful to control as a coach. In fact it was said that big Steve had knocked out a coach who had upset him. When Vince heard of this he decided to front big Steve to see about his intentions towards him. 'Are me and you going to see eye to eye Steve' asked Vince as both stood on the playing area at Central Park, 'because if we are not, we had better see who is the best man here and now.' Big Steve looked shocked but recovered quickly, 'I have no problems with you at all Vince, and can't ever see me having any' said big Steve and the two got on well.

Vince's old team mate at Saints, that tough great team man, Wilf Smith, whom I had the privilege of working with at Wigan, was coaching Blackpool Borough at this time and wanted to see how Vince and Peter Smethurst were training and preparing the first division side for matches so he asked Vince if he could come along one training session to take notes. 'Of course you can Wilf, we will be delighted to see you', so Wilf went to Central Park and was made to feel at home. Again we see the gentlemanly side of this tough legend. In this, Vince's third season at Wigan, he was pleased with the way the weights regime had taken off at the club, but he was looking to improve on the clubs league position. In his initial season the club had finished in 7th place in the league. Last season an acceptable 5th place was achieved, so if further improvement could be maintained, it may well be a place inside the top four this time. The two consistent clubs over the past few seasons had been Saints and Hull Kingston Rovers and Widnes had come like a train up the league from 10th in 1976-77 to 1st in 1977-78. Wigan had won 15 games in Vince's first season and 17 in his second. To be sure of a top four place the side had to win 20 or more games.

Vince ventured into the transfer market for Wigan when he went to Saints and bought his brother, Tony Karalius who had started his professional career at Widnes and moved to Saints to play 311 games for the Knowsley Road club. Just looking at the quality of players that Vince had at Central Park, George Fairbairn was possibly the best full-back in this country, Dennis Ramsdale and Jimmy Hornby his two regular wingmen, the centres would be from Alan Greenall, Trevor Stockley, John Butler and Kieron O'Loughlin. His half backs were selected from Martin Foy, Bernard Coyle, Les Bolton, David Walsh, O'Loughlin, Butler and Sayer. His choice of pack would be from props Breheny, Nelson, Steve O'Neill, Platt, Stephens and Regan. A fine selection of hookers included Tony Karalius, Nicky Kiss and Geoff Aspinall, whilst the second row would come from Billy Melling, Terry Hollingsworth, John Foran, utility back/forward Malcolm Swann and O'Neill. At loose forward was the redoubtable and cruel tackler, Dennis Boyd, plus Hollindsworth, Melling, John Pendlebury and young Michael Rennox. All in all, a decent squad, good key players in the right positions and above all a great leader on the bench in Vince.

The 1978-79 season began with a futile trip to the far north west to take on Workington Town in the Lancashire Cup. Town had won the County Cup the season before, beating Wigan 16–13 and the Cumbrians were still a powerful team up on the side of the Solway Firth. Wigan failed to score a try with a defeat that was a little unexpected by 14 points to 2. Tony Karalius, Vince's cousin and namesake of Vince's brother, who played at loose forward for me in my spell as Wigan's coach, actually played at full-back in the first two games of the season, the second a healthy 27 points to 10 home win over Swinton in the Floodlit Trophy.

Wigan then proceeded on a good winning run, loosing only twice, away to Bradford Northern by 19 points to 8 and away to Hull Kingston Rovers 24–17. In the ten games since the County Cup defeat at Workington, wins away at Leigh, 23–16, Wakefield Trinity, 17–3, Doncaster in the John Player 30 points to 2 and at home, Huddersfield 37–17,

Featherstone Rovers 23–14, Rochdale Hornets in the Floodlit Trophy 13–2 and Hornets again in the league, 20–10 ensured a good start to the season.

The touring Australians, skippered by the Warrington-born Bobby Fulton, visited these shores in the 1978 part of the term and what a good side they had. Vince's former Widnes player, Chris Anderson, made his first tour and dotted amongst the old stagers: Fulton, Graham Eadie, Tom Raudonikis, Steve Rogers and Mick Cronin, were the young guns: Craig Young, Ian Schubert, Les Boyd, Rod Reddy, Max Krilich and a new signing to rugby league from the Wallabies' rugby union set-up, Ray Price. A game against Wigan was scheduled for 8 November 1978 and Vince played just about his best side with his pack looking strong and mobile. His side was: Fairbairn; Ramsdale, Willicombe, Greenall, Hornby; O'Loughlin, Coyle; Wood, Tony Karalius, O'Neill, Foran, Melling and Boyd, subs: Swann and Regan. George Fairbairn kicked a penalty goal to give Wigan their only points of the game, as the Aussie tourists were too big, strong and fast for the 'Riversiders' to handle.

Two cracking wins against, Leeds, away, 23–14 and Hull Kingston Rovers, home, 21–11 with a creditable 13–all draw, away at Featherstone Rovers in between, followed the Aussie match. Then, when all looked good for Vince and his men, Wigan travelled to Keighley in the second round of the John Player Trophy. No problems, Keighley were well and truly fixed in mid table of the second division. There were several changes from the team that played Australia but it was still strong enough to beat most first division sides. But the lightning struck. Keighley played it the only way they could to get a result. They hustled and bustled and harried Wigan into mistake after mistake and even when Vince introduced the speedy Stockley and Rennox, there was no way through the staunch Yorkshire defence. Foran did crash over and Fairbairn kicked one goal. But the 9 points scored by Keighley was enough to send them into round three and Wigan, a trip back over the top licking their wounds.

As Christmas 1978 came around, the old enemy Saints were waiting at Knowsley Road for the annual derby match. Very few games hold as much fervour as this fixture and since the beginning of rugby league, this traditional game has brought the best, and the worst, out in some of the players. What an unusual time to hold 'derby' matches, the season of good will! The other traditional date for the return game is Good Friday, another day when we should all look with piety toward our fellow man, and that includes Saints players should you be a Wigan player! So Boxing Day saw Wigan arrive at Saints in the knowledge that last year the Wiganers won 22–17 over Easter but had lost last seasons Christmas fixture at Central Park, 24–13. Vince especially wanted a win as it would help erase the recent loss to Keighley. Wigan had won their last game at Fartown, Huddersfield, on 10 December 1978, by 37–13 and with three hard games before the first round of the Challenge Cup, he realised that a win over Saints would put the season back on track. But in a very hard game, Saints held all the trump cards and despite Ramsdale, Hollingsworth and Coyle scoring tries and Stockley landing a solitary goal, Saints won this important encounter 18–11.

Barrow and Wakefield Trinity were the next two league games, the trip up to Craven Park, Barrow, being particularly successful with a Wigan win, 17 points to 6. Wakefield Trinity at Central Park were a slightly tougher proposition than Barrow away. Rebuilding steadily, Trinity were coming to terms with the break up of their fabulous teams of the 1960s and early 70s. A smart workmanlike side who were holding their own in this strong First Division, Wakefield came to Central Park full of confidence but the old problem of not travelling too well caught up with them and Wigan registered a good, 13–11 win.

The Cup draw was made and would you believe, the team that stood in Wigan's way was a little team that I knew very well. In fact it was a team that I had brought together in an effort to save the proud old Halifax club. Yes, Wigan had drawn the team that I coached, Halifax. In season 1977-78 the Thrum Hallers were on the brink of collapse. Little money in the club, lights and gas turned off in the pavilion for non-payment of bills. The Brewery had refused to deliver beer as they too were not being paid. Things were so bad that Mitre Sports who had a sponsorship deal with the Rugby Football League, had stopped supplying us with footballs. New Hunslet wanted to lease Thrum Hall to play their home games there as the Greyhound Stadium, opposite Leeds United's ground was not really up to scratch. Anyway, I begged, borrowed and stole players from around the league and although nowhere near the top first division standard, we gave a lot of first division teams the 'bum's rush' and frightened one or two out of their wits. We travelled over to Wigan on the designated Sunday, a raw, bitterly cold January day. On arrival, people were milling around on the pitch and hundreds were leaving Central Park, streaming out as if at the end of a game. Vince came over to me and said, 'Sorry about this, we tried to stop you travelling but we missed you by seconds. It looks like the game is re-arranged next Wednesday night.'

We all piled onto our bus, muttering about the overtime

from work that would be missed next Wednesday, so we passed around the two bottles of sherry that football chairman, Ronnie Dobson, a great guy, always brought to 'settle our stomachs' before a game! Wednesday came around and on the Yorkshire side of the 'hill' the grounds were rock solid with ice. I phoned the Wigan club and the secretary said, 'The ground's soft, it is perfect Maurice, you can travel with confidence.'

When we arrived the ground was deserted. Vince was on the pitch and he came over to me and said, 'You won't believe this but 30 minutes ago it was soft. This frost has come with the mist and you could feel it freezing as you stood. I am terribly sorry but I was sure it was on when you travelled.' It was one of those things. We arranged to come, again, on the following Wednesday.

This time the pitch was perfect and although we lost, 9 points to 6, we all thought that it was fate that we went across to Wigan three times, the lads covered themselves with glory, and make no mistake, we could have won it in the dying seconds. This is what happened and it has taken me 26 years to get it off my chest!

Playing away from the old dressing rooms, we had the put-in at a scrum some 10 yards from the Wigan line in the left hand corner. We used a simple little move that nearly always worked. Terry Langton our tough half-back, bent to pick up the scrum heel and, without picking it up, shot around the blind side of the scrum. Dave Busfield, our loose forward, picked up the ball and made a beeline for the Wigan stand-off, O'Loughlin. Mick Blacker my skipper and stand-off, followed Busfield in and took the sweetest of passes off his hip, to scoot under the bar without a hand being laid on him. Our bench went berserk until we saw

Fred Lindop, the referee holding his hands above his head, signalling a scrum. 'What?' I yelled and walked up the touchline to ask Fred why. As I arrived opposite Fred, a look of utter dismay was across his face. He was embarrassed. He looked flustered. The knowledgeable Wigan public were booing Fred and he was still flustered. I was spitting chips and was ready to have a go at Fred but he beat me to the punch, 'Maurice, I'm sorry, I honestly thought that Terry (Langton) had dropped the ball, and I was so busy looking for it that I missed Bussy's pick up and drive.' We were out of the cup with a tremendous scalp lost. Now I can, along with Vince, shrug my shoulders and think of what might have been. The true story is relevant to Vince's book and I apologise for mentioning it in this dedication to a legend.

Because of the two postponements, Wigan had to play the second round of the Challenge Cup four days after the Halifax game. It was at Widnes and the Chemics were too strong for Vince's men and his former club beat Wigan by 21 points to 5. Widnes went on to lift the Challenge Cup by beating Wakefield Trinity at Wembley that season.

Now Vince only had the championship to aim for so it was imperative to reach as high in the league as possible to give a chance of at least a couple of home draws in the play-offs.

Researching into the reasons Vince left Central Park, the overriding issue was that whilst he maintained a top eight position for the club, his side won nothing and the Wigan supporters and board of directors were absolutely hungry for some success. Between the Challenge Cup and the end of season there were 14 league games. Unfortunately nine of those were lost. Whereas of the 16 league games before the cup ties, only four were lost and one drawn. Wigan finished in a disappointing sixth place with 33 points.

A bright spot in the league was the win over Saints at Central Park on Good Friday by 7 points to 5, Billy Melling scoring the try and George Fairbairn kicked two goals, but Widnes roasted them three times in the season, home and away in the league and at Naughton Park in the cup. Leigh won at Wigan, 13–12 and Warrington beat them 14–8 also at Wigan. Castleford and Salford did the double on them and all these were bad defeats to the men on the board.

Finishing sixth sent Wigan to Widnes in round one of the play-offs and a surprising very good win by 12 points to 8. Ramsdale and Sayer scoring tries, Fairbairn kicked two goals and Melling and Fairbairn dropped a goal each. The second round of the play-off took Vince and his men to Headingley to meet Leeds who had dispatched Saints in the first round. A defeat by 20 points to 10 ended Vince's rather disappointing season, a season that had looked so promising with the side's early league form. Vince had been in the game long enough to know how demanding clubs like Wigan were where success was concerned. Wigan yearned for the good old days of Gee, Egan, Mountford and Ryan, with major cups each season. Vince had given them consistency but no cups.

The 1979-80 season, which would ultimately end with a disastrous relegation into division two in the unheard-of demotion of this fabulous club, saw the end of Vince's reign as Wigan's supremo. No one ever said why but it must have been the combination of the Wigan board demanding the ultimate success and Vince wanting out, in equal shares. Vince left in September 1979 and the results that month were enough to sicken any coach, especially if the coach was a very proud man and would not stand for the frustration of seeing his team, week in, week out, playing without the coach's main attributes – pride and passion.

Even the greatest players and coaches can hit a barren period and this final month for Vince at the sharp end of coaching at Central Park shows the rollercoaster ride that our beloved game gives you if you stay long enough in it. Warrington were taken on at Wilderspool in the County Cup first round and although it was a close run thing, the 'Wire' were victorious by 17 points to 14. In this match there were two players with the same name, Tony Karalius. Hooker Tony, Vince's brother, and young Tony, Vince's cousin. Wakefield Trinity were next and Wigan suffered a 22–6 loss at Belle Vue. The following two games were won, Hull at Central Park, by 19 points to 15, and Pilkington Recs in the first round of the John Player, played at Knowsley Road, by 18–9. Two further losses ended the month of September, Hunslet, away, 16–10 and Castleford, away in the second round of the John Player, by 24 points to 10. Early October 1979 saw the new coach arrive at Central Park, another former Saint, Kel Coslett.

Vince went out of the game again thinking, at long last, that he was clear of rugby league and now could concentrate solely on his family. As the year progressed Vince found that he was again in demand as an after-dinner speaker and he began to enjoy the challenge that this brought. At this time Vince and Barbara had begun to think about a house in the country, well almost another country. It was on the superb Isle of Man.

On the after-dinner circuit Vince was asked by the Member of Parliament for Widnes if he would be interested in coming down to Westminster to speak, after dinner, to a group of MP's. Vince agreed and was a huge success. He was invited to take a walk up to the roof of the Palace of Westminster and he accepted. The view was magnificent but it was the fantastic leaded roof that also took Vince's breath away. The Right Honourable Gentleman from Widnes nearly fell off the roof, laughing, when Vince said, 'I know one or two lads from Widnes who would like to be up here amongst all this lead for a few minutes.'

Both Barbara and Vince were proud when youngest daughter, Stella, gained a place at Liverpool University to study to become a doctor. Stella took up residence in the Toxteth area, which at the time had a poor reputation. Vince was worried about this and took one or two quiet trips around the district to check on its security. But he needn't have worried as Stella came out of it with flying colours.

On 9 December 1981 one of Vince's fiercest opponents and dearest friends died in his early fifties. Brian McTigue, one of the most skilful handling, tough tackling and hardest props ever to grace our game. Vince thought the world of him. Vince spoke a superb endorsement of the quality of Brian McTigue when I spoke with him recently. 'I have travelled with Brian McTigue for many miles, on planes, boats, trains, almost all forms of transport and hardly three words were spoken by this quiet, hard, tough man. Yet whenever I needed help, when faced by several Australian or New Zealand irate opponents, he was always the first by my side. He was respected wherever he played as a player or went as a human being.'

Just after Brian's death, Vince heard that another of the dear friends that he made as a player was seriously ill. Bill Healey was a tough, old fashioned, respected loose forward who played at Wembley for Barrow. Vince had many a hard tussle with Bill both in league and cup football and Bill, a good Catholic lad, was one who would never give in nor call time except and until the final whistle blew. This little tale tells of the strong friendships that were forged in the red hot pitched battles that took place on the professional rugby league fields in those days now gone. It also tells of the strong faiths held by the game's players. Bill Healey's business was running a pub in Barrow. Being a former paratrooper, Bill's establishment was aptly named 'The Red Beret' and nobody messed around in Bill's pub! Vince and Barbara went across to Barrow to see Bill, who was very seriously ill indeed. Bill's wife greeted her visitors and explained that Bill had not eaten for a few days, just slept. 'Bill, here's Vince and Barbara to see you' called his wife as they went into the front room. Bill seemed to improve by the second on seeing his old adversary and talked of battles between them many years earlier. They also talked of other great players and of those tough Aussies and Kiwis they crossed swords with. But Bill tired and Vince knew it was time to leave. As they said their farewells to Bill's wife, the old Barrow forward called out to Vince to have a quiet word. 'Vince', he said, without any fear at all, 'I'll be seeing Brian (McTigue) soon and I will tell him I saw you and that you were OK'. Vince left, deeply moved at Bill's strength and faith. Bill Healey died a few days later. Poignant, but true.

In March 1983 the coach at Widnes, Doug Laughton, resigned. His assistants, the long-serving Widnes player and assistant coach, Harry Dawson and former Wigan full-back, Colin Tyrer, stood in as caretaker coaches and saw the season through to a very successful end, winning the Premiership title at Headingley by beating Hull FC, 22 points to 10. And that after two excellent wins in the play-offs, both away,

Saints 11–7 and Hull Kingston Rovers 21–10. Harry and Colin both indicated that they did not want the job as the Widnes club had decided that they wanted one coach in charge and both men did the honourable thing so as to keep equality between them. Something had to be done and quickly as the season was due to begin shortly. Vince was now living on the Isle of Man and, allowing for the travelling involved, he was contacted to see if he would be interested in becoming football manager overseeing the coaching partnership of Harry Dawson and Colin Tyrer. Vince sorted out the travel problem and agreed to return to Naughton Park. Colin Tyrer could not agree to this and resigned his position at the club, therefore leaving the door open for Harry Dawson, a long time friend of Vince's, to take on the job of first team coach, in tandem with Vince as manager. These two old mates soon had the team shipshape and the season was greeted with great expectation.

Leigh, away, and Warrington and Whitehaven at home were all beaten as they prepared to take on Vince's former club and Widnes's old enemy, Wigan, in the Lancashire Cup. An outstanding win by 36 points to 20 brought about that old feeling in the town that Vince was back! Whenever he was connected to his home town club, they did something great. Oops! A loss at Hull Kingston Rovers by 10 points to 4 brought them back to earth. Leigh, away again in round two of the County Cup and another cracking win by 27 points to 10, was followed by another league win against Salford at home, 28–14. The next game was crucial, Swinton, at Station Road in the County Cup semi-final and with a tremendous performance the Chemics stormed into the final on the back of a 22–8 win.

Now about this time I was coaching at Bramley and was

ready to quit as a new chairman usurped the club and backstabbed my chairman, Mr Douglas Alton, to remove him from the chair. I resigned in sympathy and went straight away to coach Oulton Raiders, then in the Yorkshire League. I say this because this 1983-84 season was the one that allowed me to reach for the 'big time' when I took on the coaching job at Leeds in an already long career and which brought me into opposition to Vince for the second time – the first being when I coached at Halifax in that exciting cup tie at Wigan and the 'no try' incident. Leeds played Widnes four times in this season and it appeared that we, Leeds, had the edge on Widnes, but more of that later.

Wigan were demolished at Central Park by 31 points to 16 in the league and the prelims were well and truly over as the next fixture was the big early season major final for the Lancashire Cup. The traditionally excellent side, Barrow, were the other finalists and the venue was Central Park, Wigan. Widnes were definite favourites going into this game as Harry Dawson had done a wonderful job working with the players when Vince couldn't get across the Irish Sea. The teams were at strength and started thus: Barrow: Tickle; Moore, Whittle, Ball, Milby; McConnell, Cairns; Hodgkinson, Wall, McJennett, Herbert, Szymala and Mossop. Widnes: Burke; Lydon, Hughes, O'Loughlin, Bassnett; Myler, Gregory; S O'Neill, Elwell, Tamati, Whitfield, Eric Prescott and Adams. With a Leigh-born captain and former Salford and Wigan prop and second rower, Barrow brought off a startling win against the odds and that captain, Alan Hodgkinson, was a very proud man indeed as he lifted that grand old cup. Barrow won it by 12 points to 8, with Joe Lydon scoring the four point try and also kicking two goals for Widnes and McConnell darting over for

Barrow's try, Ball kicking three goals and a drop goal and Tickle chipping in with a neat drop goal. A disappointment for Harry and Vince but both men knew there was still a lot to play for yet. Looking back on the season to date Widnes had played ten league and cup games and lost only two.

After the County Cup Final the side went on the rampage and won the next four games. Oldham away, Leigh at home, Featherstone Rovers away and Whitehaven, in the preliminary round of the John Player, away, this by 36 points to nil. Then came the first meeting with Leeds at Headingley, and a win to Leeds by 20 points to 14. As Widnes were getting back to winning ways at Belle Vue, Wakefield, with a win over Trinity, I was being interviewed the following day for the Leeds job and my first game as the Leeds coach was in the second round of the John Player, the same day that Widnes beat Bradford Northern at the same stage by the almost ridiculous score of two points to one. Steve O'Neill and Andy Gregory each dropping a goal. Hull were crushed, 30–0, at home then came two John Player games back to back. Barrow, at home were beaten 18–6, and six days later, Wigan were pipped, 20 points to 15, in a terrific nail-biter, again at Naughton Park.

Into the month of December now, with the bitter cold, icy winds and ankle deep mud on some pitches. An unexpected defeat at that most difficult place to win, Post Office Road, Featherstone by 21 points to 6, put Widnes back on their toes for the crucial John Player semi-final, played at Warrington on the 17th of the month. St Helens were their opponents and they went to Warrington to win the game. Widnes though were in no mood to be frivolous and they too set about their task with vigour. Linton and Garrity, the two speedy wingmen, dashed over for tries and Mick Burke landed five goals to put the Chemics into yet another cup final. The other semi-final was a little affair going on at Fartown, Huddersfield, between Leigh and Leeds. The Leeds side battling through, thanks to a terrific man of the match performance by Keith Rayne, who cemented a place on the 1984 tour to Australia and New Zealand with his super work rate. The results of the semi-finals read thus, Widnes 18 Saints 4 and Leeds 18 Leigh 11. The final would be played on 14 January 1984, at Central Park, Wigan.

Vince was commuting back and forth from the Isle of Man, getting over for important team meetings and to as many training sessions as he could, plus of course, all the games. The Great Britain coach at this time was Vince's cousin and great friend, Frank Myler. With Vince spending part of the week over the sea, he left all football matters with Harry Dawson, obviously talking things over with Harry about vital matters and advising Harry that he, Vince, didn't want their players being taken all over the country with the Great Britain tour selection squad for mid-week training. The problem was that Widnes were having one heck of a good season and Vince could smell something big for this particular squad of theirs and, in no way, did he want disruptions because of injury to his key players whist training with cousin Frank on Great Britain duty. Now having been in the positions of both Frank and Vince, I can tell you that it is both very worrying and frustrating, worrying as a club coach that your players will pick up an injury and frustrating for the international coach when the player's club refuse to allow him to train with the national squad. I indeed sympathise with both coaches. Vince made it clear to Harry that he did not want his key players put into the dilemma of making the choice so Vince himself laid down the rules – no Great

Britain training in the week of a big club match. Harry's problem was that with the good league winning runs, plus the good cup runs, all the Widnes games were very big ones!

With the semi-final out of the way, Vince and Harry concentrated on the League games and worried about cup finals when they came around. Bradford Northern were beaten 24–14 at Odsal and Saints were also beaten 20 points to 12 at Knowsley Road to continue their cracking league run. The next league game was at Headingley against Leeds and only six days away from the John Player final. Having won already at Naughton Park my Leeds team were as confident as one would expect, without being blasé and before a big Leeds home crowd my side managed a 17 points to 8 win. Now we come to a little anomaly between the two sets of coaching staffs. Widnes, with Vince and Harry had a wealth of successful cup final experience behind them. Leeds had me as coach, going into only my second ever professional cup final as my own man. I had been assistant coach at Dewsbury with Tommy Smales when we went to the Yorkshire Cup final in 1972 and were beaten well by Leeds. As my own man we went in 1979 to the County Cup final with my Halifax side and were beaten, again by Leeds. So, in the coaching stakes, we were up against it. On the positive side, we had beaten Widnes twice that season, but some would say that we were then two games nearer being beaten!

I remember all too well that Saturday afternoon. It had snowed all morning in Leeds and I remember the team bus sliding and skidding sideways as we pulled out of the Headingley ground into St Michaels Lane. The trip along the M62 to Wigan was horrendous with abandoned cars left in snow drifts along the hard shoulder of the motorway. A gale was blowing too and news came over the bus radio from Radio Leeds that the set of posts at the dressing room end of Central Park had blown down in the gales overnight. The Wigan ground staff managed to save one post and the cross bar but the other post had broken in two. They had worked since early morning to erect a half post in the broken one's place so the posts did not create a problem. But gales, snow flurries and a freezing wind greeted the teams as they came out onto the sodden, but playable, Central Park pitch and I was a worried man as Widnes threw the ball about as if it was August instead of the most miserable winter's day. It became worse for the Leeds bench as the ball was transferred to Ralph Linton, who made try scoring look simple, as he scorched over to open the scoring. But with David Ward, Man of the Match Mark Laurie and the Rayne twins, Keith and Kevin, blocking the middle and those two experienced half-backs John Holmes and Kevin Dick working well, Leeds hit back and although Joe Lydon scored another try for Widnes and Mick Burke kicked a goal, tries by Holmes and Dick, plus five David Creasser goals paved the way for an 18–10 Leeds win and allowed me my first cup final success. This was three out of three for Leeds, home and away in the league and this major success, but I would have swapped all three wins for three loses to have won our fourth encounter of the season with the very dangerous Chemics.

Back onto the league grind and Vince saw the next two games end in victory as Widnes took care of Whitehaven away, 18–4, and Castleford at home, 14–8, before beginning another Wembley charge. Another preliminary round had to be played when Vince took his men up to Cumbria to face lowly Carlisle. They came away with a win by 20 points to 12, then it was the cup again a week later when Dewsbury were the visitors to Naughton Park. The Crown Flatts men were beaten heavily by 54 points to 10. Wakefield Trinity were the next to feel the power of Widnes when they lost by a big margin, 42–14, and the next game was a tough and dangerous away trip to the fledgling newcomer in London, Fulham, who were coached by the former Widnes favourite, Reg Bowden. It was a tough one as expected and Widnes scraped home by 12 points to 10 – a close run thing.

Widnes were due a defeat, they had gone six tough games unbeaten. They came a cropper away to Hull at the Boulevard by 30 points to 12. A request for all players selected for Great Britain to be allowed to train with the international squad on one session per week was not accepted by Vince as his thoughts on the matter have been mentioned earlier. Hull Kingston Rovers came to Widnes in the third round of the Challenge Cup and they were riding high at the top of the table. Widnes, playing superb cup tie football, won by 21–10, but the following mid-week the Rovers of East Hull came again in the league to Widnes and won handsomely, 17–8, and Widnes were without key half-back Andy Gregory.

It was now that the friendship of Vince and Harry split after years of being close mates. Before returning home to the Isle of Man this particular week, Vince reiterated to Harry his requirement of not allowing players to go to international training. As football manager Vince had the overall say on team matters. He returned to Widnes for the mid-week game against Hull Kingston Rovers only to find that Andy Gregory had been allowed to train with the Great Britain squad and had received a leg injury which would keep him out of this crucial League game. Vince and Harry had a meeting and Vince again told his old mate what he had wanted and why did Harry allow Andy Gregory to go. 'Come on Vince, I am the coach after all and I said it would be OK,' argued Harry. 'No, Harry, I am the manager and lay down the rules and regulations,' Vince told him. With this bust up, Harry Dawson resigned from the coach's job. The loss of his mate was a blow to Vince but the club were well set for Wembley, only one club stood in their way in the semi-final at Swinton and Vince wanted Wembley again for his home town club. Oh yes, the team they had drawn was Leeds.

Vince stayed on to see the job through. During the upset of Vince and Harry's fall out, Reg Bowden brought his Fulham team back home to Widnes and beat his former club, 16–14, but Vince had the side back on the winning habit with a good 22–12 win away at Salford on the Friday evening, eight days before the semi-final. The build-up to the game from my memory was that Leeds trained at Scarborough Football Club on the Thursday prior to the game and that week we were hit by several key injuries. Widnes were going to be harder to beat in this game as their pride would be on the line after three consecutive defeats. The key men out for us were my captain and superb leader, David Ward, the outstanding forward all season Mark Laurie and the ebullient Roy Dickinson.

On the day we were outplayed in every department and in Kevin Tamati and the hard grafting Steve O'Neill leading the way in the pack and Tony Myler and Andy Gregory – superb at half-back making the backs tick – we were up against it from the start. Joe Lydon's long range try when he took the ball from Tamati, kicked over our full-back, Ian Wilkinson, re-gathered and sprinted over from 60 yards was a brilliant effort. Vince had done it again with his Wembley 'touch'. It is also strange how people's paths cross and counter cross in our game. Vince had coached at Wigan, I had coached at Wigan and it was Wigan who had gone through to Wembley first when the week before our semi-final, Wigan had beaten York at Elland Road in a rain ruined first semi-final.

But the league continued and Bradford Northern had to be mastered at home, and were with a 32–23 win but then Oldham travelled to Widnes four days later and the Roughyeds won, 34–28. A reminder that these games were not Sunday to Sunday matches with a full week's rest in between, they were played, around the end of season usually, Wednesday, then Sunday and the fixtures repeated on those days until all league games had been played. For instance, Widnes played Leeds in the Challenge Cup semi-final on Saturday 31 March, and then 4 April they played Bradford Northern. On 8 April they played Oldham and on the 11th played Wigan at home and won 21–14, on the 15th Widnes made the trip to Wheldon Road, Castleford and lost 24–18, and five days later recorded a resounding win at Wilderspool by 36–16. Three days later they took on the mighty Saints at home and earned a creditable 28–all draw on the 23rd and the crunch game came when a tired out Widnes travelled to the capital to play Reg Bowden's Fulham on the 25th only to lose, 23–13. So in the 25 days since Widnes played in the cup semi-final, they played seven games and with the top eight play-off at Castleford on 29 April, Vince's team had played eight games from the 4th to the 29th of April.

With Wembley being on 5 May, to ask the Widnes side to go to Castleford only six days before the final was indeed a very big ask and the result was a foregone conclusion with a massive win by 36–4 to Castleford. Widnes completed their league programme and finished in fifth place, the same as the previous season, with 19 wins, 1 draw and 10 losses. They ended up with 39 points in the table, the same as Castleford but with an inferior points average, for and against.

So Vince had his former club Wigan to plot against in the final. And who was the man plotting against him? Why it was his old buddy from his Saints and Great Britain days, the one and only Alex Murphy, who was then the coach at Wigan. History certainly repeated itself as the two old friends were in opposition at the 1975 Wembley final too, when Vince was in his first coaching stint at Widnes and Alex was the coach at Warrington. On that occasion Widnes were the victors by 14 points to 7.

Vince continued his old routine of training a few days at Southport before journeying down to Wembley and the side were in a confident mood as they embarked for their hotel on Thursday of cup final week. Vince had under his charge two of the brightest stars our game had produced for many years in the lightning quick Joe Lydon and the little general and king-pin half-back, Andy Gregory. Added to these two was a mobile pack that included the tough New Zealand international, Maori Warrior Kevin Tamati, the brothers Mike and Steve O'Neill and that grand footballer Mick Adams. The full line-ups read thus: Widnes: Burke; Wright, Hughes, Lydon, Basnett; O'Loughlin, Gregory; S O'Neill, Elwell, Kevin Tamati, Gorley, M O'Neill and Adams. Subs: Hulme and Whitfield. Wigan: Edwards; Ramsdale, Stephenson, Whitfield, Gill; Cannon, Stephens; Hemsley, Howie, Tamati, Case, West, Scott and Pendlebury. Subs: Elvin and Juliff. The attendance was 80,116 and it was a trade mark show of power by Widnes that took the game away from Wigan.

Joe Lydon scorched in for two tries and his all-round display won him the coveted Lance Todd Trophy for best player of the match, Keiron O'Loughlin added another great try and Mick Burke landed three goals. Master drop goal specialist Steve O'Neill chipped in with a neat drop goal to give Widnes their 19 points and Wigan's answer was a Kerry Hemsley try and a Colin Whitfield goal for their six points. There were wonderful scenes at Wembley after the game as the Widnes team celebrated yet another Challenge Cup success and Vince's mind must have stretched back over the years to his seven visits to the Twin Towers. His first as a travelling reserve as a rookie kid in the 1953 Huddersfield v Saints game, 'Ramsden's Final' as it is remembered and a 15–10 defeat. Then the Saints v Halifax 1956 game with Vince receiving his first winners medal. The very enjoyable win over Wigan in 1961 for Saints, followed by the superb victory as captain of Widnes in 1964 against Hull Kingston Rovers and the two successful visits as first coach of Widnes in 1975 against Warrington, now this great victory as manager/coach against the terrific club Wigan. The other time Vince played at Wembley was for Great Britain in the defeat by the Aussies by 28 points to 2 in October 1963.

Vince's record of seven visits to Wembley and only two defeats is something very special and this latest win was extra special to him as his home town club managed a win against one of his former coaching employers. Vince was appointed again for the following year but on reflection he considered the continual travelling, the time away from family and home and the enforced pressures of the job, plus the fact that the team needed a coach who was on the job, near to the club and could get there at a few minutes' notice. So he met with the Widnes committee and in the most amicable way moved over to allow Eric Hughes to take over for the new season as coach, with that great clubman, Mal Aspey, as his assistant. It was also decided to dispense with the position of team manager and allow the new coach to cover both jobs. Vince agreed and offered his services any time as an advisor to Eric Hughes.

Vince retired at last. His legacy at Saints as a player and at Widnes as a player, coach and administrator, is there to see to this day. He was ensconced in the St Helens Hall of Fame for his outstanding services to that great club, and another huge accolade was awaiting him in the year 2000 when on the occasion of the World Cup Final, Vince was introduced as one of the three new members of the Rugby League Hall of Fame. Tom Vollenhoven and Roger Millward joined Vince to make the number of all time stars, thirteen. In 2005 a further four ex-players were inducted into the Hall of Fame: Ellery Hanley, Douglas Clark, Martin Hodgson and Eric Ashton. Clark and Hodgson were 'pure' forwards like Vince, Hanley played a great deal of his football in the backs and like Neil Fox, is remembered more for his achievements as a centre, although he did move into the pack in his final years as a player, but Vince started and finished as a back row forward.

Vince's career began in the early 1950s and continued, as a player, into the middle 1960s, always at the top level. Because of his involvement over 50 years ago, the inevitable question arises, 'Would he have been such a big star in today's game?' Well, that of course is impossible to answer, but certain comparisons can be made and the reader can make up his or her own mind.

CONCLUSIONS AND COMPARISONS

In every sport we make comparisons. Of players, of managers systems, of game plans. Is so and so a better player than you know who? Was such a player as good as today's players? In soccer, the ability to play and entertain the spectators hasn't changed all that much from the middle of the last century. We still speak with reverence of Stanley Matthews, Tom Finney, Bobby Charlton, George Best, Trevor Brooking and 'Dixie' Dean. Are they as good as Wayne Rooney or David Beckham? Is Michael Vaughan as good as Len Hutton? Flintoff as good as Botham? Are Harmison and Hoggard as good as Trueman and Statham? Would Rocky Marciano have stood up to Lennox Lewis? The list is endless. But apart from a few law and rule changes, these sports have hardly changed at all. The game of rugby league football changed out of all proportion in the mid 1990s with the introduction of Super League. Not only did we move, lock, stock and barrel from your traditional winter sport to a summer game, we took the proud old system of part time professionalism, threw it away, and introduced full-time professionals at every Super League club. After 100 years of struggle, against the far wealthier 15-a-side handling code and the nation's national winter sport, soccer, we finally made it into the big time. And this is why comparisons of players pre- and post-Super League are so difficult.

Imagine the difference, a player having to hold down a regular nine to five job, then, going to train for two hours on Tuesday and Thursday evenings in the rain, sleet, freezing winds and even snow in the middle of winter. There were very few club gymnasiums and very few weights training facilities. Fitness was achieved by running, running and more running. Skills drills were a thing of the future as were most forms of weights work. Most clubs were on the verge of bankruptcy. Ends were met and bills were paid by selling on a couple of your better players to wealthier clubs in an archaic player transfer system. But at least money used to circulate around the clubs and the sale of one good prospect would ensure financial security for at least twelve months. A newfangled idea arose called a 'youth policy', whereby youngsters teams were started within the professional clubs and the best talent was signed on – usually for peanuts – and groomed for stardom. OK, we needed to change but when change came, it was awesome. As described, players suddenly found themselves in full-time employment as our beloved, traditional game swung, decidedly, towards the Australian system. Full-time employment meant full-time training, going to the club training ground daily, to pump iron and work on fitness and skills. Defence, handling, game awareness, pre-match personal preparation and all the things that the Aussies learned from American grid iron football, then passed on to us mainly via the flood of overseas players who arrived about the same time as the money from SkyTV, Super League's biggest sponsor.

So, taking all this into account, let us consider if we think that Vince Karalius would have held his own in today's football. Let's look at what was against him first. I don't think his physical size would be a problem, he was very fit for his day and he would not have reduced his weight by modern day training as he was doing this type of conditioning in his own time. Playing at loose forward today one can get by at around 14 to 15 stones if everything else is in the correct place!

His pace? Well, being full time and with the expert advisers on sprinting, cadence, and balance, I think Vince may well have put a yard or two on and that would have been enough.

His courage and defensive ability? Don't let us talk silly!

His attitude to discipline? Same as the last question! Treat him as Jim Sullivan did, just let him play!

What would he have going for him, the first thing to ask, can he play? Just a bit!

Would he ever let you down if the going got tough? Don't be daft!

Was he skilful enough? Will the Sun rise tomorrow?

Was he a leader of men? Was Alexander the Great (and not Murphy) a leader of men?

I know, after all the accolades that one still can not be certain that all the tumblers that dropped into place for Vince in his day, would drop into place today. But the same can be said for all of yesterday's great players, Alex Murphy, Dick Huddart, Tom Vollenhoven, Willie Horne, Billy Boston, Mick Sullivan, Eric Ashton, Lewis Jones, Arthur Clues, Dave Valentine, Gerry Helme, Martin Ryan, Brian Bevan, Brian McTigue and hundreds more. The players from our golden age, just how good would they have been under today's regime? Boston on the charge was as dangerous as any in the game today, Jones was magic on his day, Huddart virtually unstoppable, Murphy, bloody brilliant, we could go on forever. The end product is, would they have fitted in with the modern game? I for one feel they would. In this age when we have suddenly discovered the kicking game, who remembers when Murphy changed the laws of the game 40 years ago because he could kick so well, who could kick more accurately than Jimmy Ledgard of Dewsbury, Leigh and

Great Britain? Not many. Freddy Miller of Hull and Featherstone Rovers would have loved these 40/20s, he could back-heel a 40/20! He could have hit a 40/20 the length of Salisbury Plain!

The era of Vince Karalius was blessed by brilliant loose forwards. Not all had the silky smooth skills of Billy Blan (Wigan) or the stand up, knock 'em over defence of Bill Hudson (Batley and Wigan). Not all had the pace of Ike Owens (Leeds, Huddersfield, Castleford and Great Britain), or Roy Evans (Wigan and Great Britain). Not all had the pure leg tackling skill or the immaculate handling ability of the classical Ken Traill (Hunslet, Bradford Northern, Halifax, Wakefield Trinity and Great Britain). Who else but 'Gentleman' Johnny Whiteley (Hull and Great Britain) had the robust, sheer athleticism of such a big man? Who could match the outstanding toughness and footballing ability of Derek 'Rocky' Turner (Hull KR, Oldham, Wakefield and Great Britain)? Who could ever overcome the strength, dedication and total unacceptability of defeat that was Vince Karalius (Saints, Widnes and Great Britain)? Some of the loose forwards mentioned were approaching retirement as Vince started but the wealth of number 13s in and around in those early 1950s was tremendous. Des Clarkson (Hunslet, Leigh, Leeds, Halifax, Keighley), Billy Iveson (Workington Town), Harry Street (Dewsbury, Wigan, Leeds), Bryn Goldswain (Oldham), Bill Healey (Barrow), Cliff Lambert (Featherstone Rovers) Arthur Bedford (Hull), and Harold Palin (Warrington) were just some of the excellent men around.

So, was there a player of the opposition whom Vince didn't particularly get on with? Given that rugby league is such a physical game were there players around who could intimidate him or wind him up? One player who seemed to always make a bee-line for Vince was Jack Wilkinson of Halifax, then Wakefield Trinity. Vince and Jack once had a real set-to in a match when big Jack, doing his job in those days, caught a Saints player a beauty and laid him out. Vince was straight into Jack and by all accounts had the big prop spread-eagled on the ground with Vince on top knocking the corners off him! Peter Dimond, the Aussie test player was another that stirred Vince up with his foul tackles on smaller men. Rex Mossop the big Aussie test forward, who had a spell at Leigh, was one of Vince's antagonists. But it was his defence of his teammates that was one of the many reasons why his colleagues respected him so highly. One former player said openly, that 'Whenever you played in the same team as Vince, you felt safe'. What a superb thing for any player to say about a team mate, you 'felt safe' with him! The late, great Eddie Waring said, in his foreword to Vince's 1964 autobiography, *Lucky Thirteen*, 'Wherever rugby league is played Vince Karalius needs no introduction. He is known throughout the rugby league world that stretches from New Zealand and Australia to the home of the game in Lancashire, Yorkshire and Cumberland. Such is the Karalius style of play that the Aussies tagged him, "The Wild Bull of the Pampas", and the Aussies don't play their football like a bunch of delirious debs! He is a star of a mans game. A game that is played by men. Tough men. Fiery, fearless, fantastic Karalius. The man the fans love, or love to hate. Vince Karalius will fill a ground with screaming spectators and he is a star in his very own right.'

To make comparisons between Vince and other loose forwards is easy. One simply asks, 'Is he as good as Vince Karalius?' Vince is the yardstick. He is the marker that others are measured by. How does one measure a legend? His deeds of valour precede him, the stories of his heroism on the field of play are told to youngsters by their dads and granddads. The conclusions are that Vince Karalius would have become a legend at whatever sport he had chosen and whether he was playing today or fifty years ago.

Luckily for followers of the greatest game, he chose the greatest game in the world, rugby league football and our game is so much richer for his presence.

AUTHOR'S TRIBUTE

The publisher of this book, Karl Waddicor, of Vertical Editions did me a tremendous service when he contacted me and asked if I would write about the football side of Vince Karalius's life. Karl found for me a copy of *Lucky Thirteen*, Vince's autobiography, via the internet. The only copy available was in a bookshop in Townsville, North Queensland!

Speaking to Vince by phone at his home in the Isle of Man was indeed a pleasure and Barbara, his wife, was always a tremendous help too.

Vince's admission to Rugby League's Hall of Fame in the year 2000, as the only one 'pure' forward of the thirteen then members, was testimony to this man's ability. When as a kid of seventeen years old I signed for Hull FC, we played in the A team on Saturday afternoons and my late dad was an avid Leeds RLFC supporter. If Leeds were at home he would go up to Headingley and support his long time team, if they were away, he would come to watch us play. He always gave me a report on how Leeds had gone on and I remember him telling me of this youngster who had played at loose forward for Saints. My dad said, 'He has an unusual name but he is going to be a cracking player!' That youngster was indeed Vincent Karalius and believe me my old dad could pick a good player out. He always used to say when Vince had made it and was playing for Great Britain, 'There you are, I told you about this lad years ago'.

To speak to Vince, or even to be in his company, gives one the feeling of being near a special presence, a legend, for that is what Vince Karalius is and the first man to deny this would be the man himself. I always thought that there was an air of mystery around certain aspects of Vince's career. When one remembers his tremendous displays, season in, season out, mainly for St Helens in a particularly successful period of their history, and the impact he made at Widnes when he arrived there and the fact that his career spanned 12 seasons at the top, yet he made only one tour and only played in half the test matches of his most fierce competitor, Derek Turner. Vince played in 12 tests and Derek in 24. Johnny Whiteley played in 15 tests, three more than Vince. The thing that I find strange is that after the 1958 tour, the Australians appeared to be running scared of Vince, yet when again he out toughed them in the 1960 World Cup along with Derek Turner and Joby Shaw, Jack Wilkinson, Brian Shaw and Brian McTigue he was ignored by the selectors for the 1962 tour. What was it that denied Vince more caps than his 12? What was it caused his non selection on the 1962 tour? The age in which Vince played is accepted as the era in which we produced a glut of world class number 13s and this could be the reason, a lot of good ones about. But his exclusion on the 1962 tour, even though we had an excellent Australian part, was hard to swallow. Could it be that someone caused problems for Vince after that 'bumpy' 1958 tour? Did someone point the finger at Vince for being outspoken on how the staff treated the players like children or being late once after curfew? I know that in those days sometimes players were 'black balled' for things like tours but in Vince's case we may never know! One thing is certain, even in today's high profile game, a young Vince Karalius would secure a place in any team in Super League as he had that vital ingredient on top of fitness, ball skills, pace and determination, that of star quality. And listening to his former teammates and opponents speak now, many years after his retirement as a player, the respect and admiration still shines through for him.

We speak a lot about Vince Karalius the player and successful business man but what about Vince Karalius, the coach? Vince as we know coached at two clubs, Widnes and Wigan. Two great rugby league clubs but as different in their ways as chalk and cheese. Widnes, the close-knit local family club who had a proud record of being able to build up excellent sides on young local talent. Wigan, mighty for many years, one of the leading clubs in the county of Lancashire. Widnes of course were not the only club to 'raise its own' as the superb Leigh, so long under the shadow of near neighbours Wigan, produced great players from the local amateur teams around their district, as did Warrington, Oldham and Swinton. But it was the big spending clubs such as Wigan and Salford who caught the eye by signing top rugby union and overseas players in those days. Vince Karalius showed his ability to be able to impose his personality on to both the clubs at which he coached, despite the difference in rugby league cultures. In one article given to a local newspaper when in his early days at Widnes, he stated that he wanted to see his home town team in the top bracket of the game with a ground to equal Headingley, Central Park and The Willows. Widnes achieved that dream, albeit a few years after Vince had finally left them, and the foundation was dug by Vince's arrival back at the club in the 1960s. Vince's work was continued by the excellent Frank Myler, Doug Laughton and of course Eric Hughes, but the outstanding success for the Widnes club, known for many seasons as the 'Cup Kings', began with the coaching career, at Naughton Park of Vince Karalius.

A lot was written at the time and a lot has been said since about the well debated fall out between Vince and his long time mate, Harry Dawson, when both men had big parts to play in the successful runs to Wembley in 1975 and 1984. The difference of opinion between the late lamented Harry Dawson and Vince was sorted out and forgotten before Harry passed away. The pair were friends again. Vince knew the team was in good hands whist he was living across the water, otherwise he would have changed things when he took the job.

Vince did the job at Widnes both as a coach and as a manager, again two vastly varying roles, just to show his versatility. His abilities did not stop at coaching or at managerial level, he was also a top class trainer, or as they say today, a conditioner (although being of the old school I always think of medication for dogs when trainers are called that). He was the first rugby league player to use weights on a regular basis in his fitness programme that I ever knew of. He was also, and this shows how advanced he was in the use of mental preparation, one of the first to use the 'see yourself doing it' system of the pre-match thought process. Vince was more down to earth and called it a hate campaign. But what Vince was doing in the early 1950s, was supposedly thought of by the American psychology guru's of professional grid iron football later in the 1960s. Vince was in front of his time with that too.

His prowess as a top player helped him in coaching immensely. Who wouldn't take notice of advice from a man of his world standing in the game? But I think he would have captured his audience no matter what the sport or what he had done before. He was, I think, the kind of personality that comes around only once in a lifetime. A player you would have loved to play alongside and a coach you would have loved to play for, that I consider the greatest accolade of all. And that sentiment is, I am certain, endorsed by all who know him, including Rex Mossop, Peter Dimond and Jean Barthe!

THEY SAID IT

Ray French (St Helens, Widnes, Lancashire, Great Britain, England rugby union)

Even though I played rugby union when I went to grammar school, joined St Helens RUFC, played at University and finally for England, my early days were all filled with rugby league. We lived just below the Knowsley Road ground and I used to watch my heroes at St Helens on every occasion that I could. Vince Karalius was the biggest of my heroes. Not just physically big but big in character and presence. Watching him as a youngster I was filled with awe at the way he created openings with the ball in those huge hands and the way that he stopped dead any attack near to him with precision bone shaking man and ball tackles. Yet, for all the many stories regarding Vince's hard, relentless toughness during a game, he was, and is, a gentleman, a courteous man and a gracious man. Because of his toughness too, people sometimes don't realise the depth of knowledge of the game that he possesses. Vince is articulate when talking about the game. He was a thinker and had a super tactical awareness about rugby league football.

I remember signing for Saints in August 1961. As I walked towards the ground at Knowsley Road, I suddenly felt nervous, very nervous, as I was about to walk into a dressing room full to the brim with international players but more to the point, two players whom I admired more than any other two, Vince Karalius and Tom Van Vollenhoven. I paced up and down that area outside the dressing rooms until I plucked up enough, I think the word would be, courage, to enter the holy of holies, the Saints heartbeat, the dressing room. The first man to me, with hand outstretched, was Vince, the second, Tom, and one would have thought that I had been there for years. I had one full season with Vince before he was transferred to Widnes and the encouragement and sound advice Vince passed on to me was mind blowing. He was one of the first in the game to realise the absolute necessity of weight training and actually had a set of weights made for me, which are still in my mum's garden shed!

Vince introduced weights for the first time to both Widnes and Wigan's training routines when he coached there and his intimidating, yet, gentle way he had in explaining the workings of what he was wanting made training and playing in the same side so enjoyable. Vince looked after you on the field, he made you feel safe. The adulation I held him in since childhood turned to overwhelming respect. He was so fit and strong, so fearless, such a great footballer, so physically hard and although all these things, plus the most intimidating man during a game that I have ever met, he was scrupulously fair! Look after himself, yes, dirty, never! Coming from rugby union and being a school teacher, I envisaged being compromised in this game of tough rugby league men, even though my dad was a very good amateur player at UGB and in fact captained the club. And the pack I played in at Saints showed the variety of jobs the blokes did as well as play at the weekend, Ab Terry (miner), Bob Dagnall (joiner), Cliff Watson (drayman), Dick Huddart (miner), Ray French (schoolteacher), Vince Karalius (scrap dealer), my profession was not a problem.

After Vince had moved to Widnes came the next unusual hurdle to overcome, that of playing against this icon, this figurehead, this almost father figure. The first time I opposed Vince in a Saints v Widnes game I wondered what to expect! Knowing Vince's likes of turning up at the last second for a game it was secretly hoped that he might miss the time of kick-off. But no, there he was, as large as life and his first hit on me, down the best stand side at Knowsley Road, told me there was no place 'for old time's sake' in Vince's locker. Bang, ball and all, with everything shaken. A real bone cruncher. So I knew then what to expect from my hero. After the game we were back as if he were still at Saints.

It is my pleasure to know, have played alongside and played against Vince, a great player, a gentleman, a real character and a legend of our game. **Ray French.**

Austin Rhodes (St Helens, Lancashire, Great Britain)

One of the things I remember about Vince was his obsession with fitness. He was fanatical. He was one of the first players that not only trained right, he ate right as well. He was always coming up with this diet or that diet, anything that would make him stronger and fitter than anyone else. In those days when you travelled away there was always a meal at a good hotel after the match. If the meat was steak, cut beef or pork, Vince would cut away all the fat and never touch it. Our coach, Jim Sullivan, used to say to Vince, 'You need a bit of that fat for your strength', but Vince would stick to his eating habits.

Vince was a devil for arriving late on match days. He drove the coach wild sometimes as he would leave it to the last minute before striding through the dressing room door. That was his way though and he was always the last man out onto the field. I was playing scrum-half and was club captain when Jim Sullivan had a word in my ear. I had been through a tough spell with a hard knock or two and lost a touch of pace with the injuries. Jim told me that he thought a change of position might help me over this sticky patch and that he would like me to consider playing at full-back. After a bit of thought I said yes. Three weeks later Jim suggested that the captain was out of the game too much and said that he would like Vince, at loose forward, to skipper the side and that is how he came to be the club captain and what a great job he did. The only thing he didn't like was that now he had to be first man onto the field.

Vince never ever looked on the game of rugby league as a game. It was war for 80 minutes, complete and utter war, with no prisoners. And in this war he held two jobs. Firstly he was the general, the boss, the governor, the enforcer. Secondly and possibly more than a general, he was a warrior! During the entire game Vince was aggressive and totally confrontational, he never relaxed for a second, it wasn't in his nature. In his younger days Vince was a bit high spirited, a bit wild, yet he controlled this rock hard temperament on the field of play as he was sent off on only a very few occasions but preparing for really big games Vince would start boiling on the morning of the match. In 1956 we at Saints played Halifax at Wembley in the Challenge Cup final. The usual pre big match rituals were carried out in that the cup final squad went to Southport on the Monday of cup final week and stayed there until we went down to a hotel in Richmond, very near to the Stadium at Wembley. On the Wednesday, Jim Sullivan allowed us to go in to Southport for a break from training. Vince and I were walking round the fair ground and we came across the gypsy fortune teller. In we both went and the gypsy touched us on the shoulder, looked in to our eyes and said, 'I can see you both holding something silver in the air'. We couldn't believe it; it had to be the cup! We went down to Richmond on the Thursday and went through the time honoured routine of visiting Wembley on the Friday. No one knew it but our opponents, Halifax, were staying in Richmond too and when on Friday afternoon Vince and I were out for a walk and a coffee, we bumped into my one-on-one opponent, Stan Keilty and Vince's arch enemy, big Jack Wilkinson. Vince started his psychological war there and then. He confronted Keilty and said, 'If you come around my blind side tomorrow, I'll pick you up and throw you over the stand'. To this threat to his scrum-half big Jack took offence and told Vince in no uncertain terms what he would do with him. 'Lets see what you've got Wilky, here and now' replied Vince and squared up to the big prop. I managed to part them and we went for our beverage. Vince and I used to be boozing partners after matches but I think he became teetotal as he never bought a round!

When he was in the army he fancied himself as a boxer and in the 1960 World Cup he proved his point as against France at Swinton, in the 33 points to 7 win, Vince and the French captain, Jean Barthe were sent off, in a turbulent game, after a fight erupted and Monsieur Barthe was decidedly the worse for wear. Then in the final against Australia at Odsal, Vince was involved in a toe to toe no holds barred bump off with the big Aussie, Rex Mossop, who left the field horizontal and feet first.

I remember Vince's pride and joy was a little Maserati car and one day we were out and about when, in the centre of St Helens the damned thing broke down and we had to push it – amid catcalls from the Saints fans – to a secure place. Very embarrassing. After matches he used to like letting his hair down with a few drinks, then after a while, it would start, his singing was atrocious. He could only murder two songs as those were the only songs he knew, 'Mardi Gras' and 'Your mother's love is a blessing' and he always finished the night with the latter. The tears ran down his face as he sang the sad song and everyone else cried too but because of the noise he was making, not the lyrics.

I think the secret of his success as a rugby league player was because of his mental and physical toughness. His presence lifted any team he played with and as a pal and a team leader he was the best. *Austin Rhodes.*

Brian McGinn (St Helens RLFC)

I was fortunate enough to play in the same great side at Saints with Vince when I was still a very young player. His leadership qualities, in one of the biggest games in my career, could be seen in the 1961 Wembley Challenge Cup final against Wigan. He was awesome. He was everywhere on the field, he covered every blade of that Wembley turf. Our win against Wigan by 12 points to 6 was a lot down to Vince; he had a blinder that day.

Another match that stood out for me was the Championship Final at Odsal against a really good Hunslet team. Vince took that game by the scruff of the neck too, he was amazing. His determination to win was so intense that you could actually feel it when you stood near him, fantastic. I had watched him, when I was a kid supporting Saints and actually remember him coming home on weekend leave from the army to play at the club. He had the ability to give you confidence during a game, with a quiet word, an arm around your shoulder or a smack on the back with a sharp,

'Well done young 'un'. He was, without doubt, the most inspirational player I have ever seen or played alongside.

I signed for Saints as a sixteen-year-old from Blackbrook ARLFC and didn't know what to expect going that first night to Knowsley Road. Jim Sullivan was the coach and he was a hard man who knew the game inside out. Vince was a gentleman to me from day one, and would go out of his way to make things right for you. As a young kid making my way in the learning stakes of top rugby league, to play with great players like Vince, Dick Huddart, Tom Vollenhoven, Alex Murphy, Wilf Smith and the rest, it was amazing to pick so much up from them about how to play the game at this level. There were a lot of tough, rough and ready lads playing then too but to see Vince come on to the field and do his usual warm up run around the part of the pitch behind the Saints team filled one with utter confidence, the main thing too is that, would you believe, you felt somehow safe with Vince being on the pitch.

After every away game the team bus would drop us off in the Town square and we would call in for a few pints into the Royal. Vince liked a good drink after a game, especially when we had won, and had a repertoire of songs, most sung badly, which he would subject us to, the favourite one was 'Down by the old mill stream'.

Without saying anything against Vince, there were a few better pure footballers than him but there was not one with a greater desire to win, or as supremely fit as him or with his leadership qualities. He was always, always sure of making plenty of full and half breaks in any match and his ability to slip out those around-the-player one-handed passes was phenomenal. Vince was very much like our coach, Jim Sullivan. Vince hated the type of player who would take 'cheap' shots at another player. He only had time for the player who 'got back on his feet and had a go'. I remember playing in one match and the tough international forward, Brian Shaw, ex Hunslet and Leeds, roughed me up in a tackle. Brian bounced me up and down like a ball and although he was two or three stones heavier than me, I manage to jump back onto my feet and actually hit him with a great punch. Big 'Shawy' walked through my best punch and just when it appeared that I may be in a spot of bother, whoosh, Vince was by my side and I had no further trouble with big Brian! Of the local Lancashire forwards, Vince rated Wigan's Brian McTigue and the Widnes forward, Edgar Bate as two of the toughest and Charlie Winslade and Sid Little, both of Oldham plus Stan Owen of Leigh all in the same category. I do know that Vince and big Jack Wilkinson had many a ding-dong between them and there never was a Halifax v Saints game when the two of them were not at it! To mention big Jack in front of Vince prior to a Halifax game was like waving a red flag at a bull. He motivated everyone, his pent up aggression before a match acted like a shot of adrenaline to us and he gave you the feeling that you could not loose.

Vince Karalius was brilliant to me both on and off the field all the time I was at Saints. His sense of humour, his pre-match behaviour and his downright refusal to be beaten was the flag by which we all rallied. Because of his all-out endeavours during a match, he took on injuries that only his personal superb fitness helped him overcome and many times Jim Sullivan would talk Vince into playing even though he should have rested. Vince had a lot of trouble with fluid around his elbows, caused by the way he ran at tacklers, worked his arms free to go around the tackler to pass the ball and nine times out of ten, he would land heavily on those sore elbows. Jim would tell him, 'They will be all right once we get kicked off' and Vince would play.

It is impossible for me to say just what I feel about Vince as a footballer and a human being. The only thing I can say is that he was great on both counts, bloody great!
Brian McGinn

Wilf Smith (St Helens RLFC)

A few months ago, I was asked to do a commentary on a Saints home game and at half time the three men involved in the broadcast were asked one question and we had to give our honest answer. The question was: 'You have one million to spend on one player. Who would that player be?' I was first on and I never hesitated at all, 'Vince Karalius,' I said. He was and is an outstanding man. As tough as old boots, tougher in fact, the best leader of men I have ever known.

I don't know anyone who knows and has played in the same team as him that doesn't rate him. Yes, he made his share of mistakes because he was always in the game. When the going was tough, the dummy half would hear a growl, 'Give it t'me', and the dummy half would see it was Vince coming for the ball, no matter how hard it was. Hard as iron though he was, I once saw big Charlie Winslade of Oldham down Vince twice in a short period of time. Charlie was a master of just catching a player at the right time with his big shoulder, under the short ribs. He caught Vince and down he went on his haunches, wheezing and blowing. I went over to him to make sure he was OK, but as I arrived Vince muttered weakly but threateningly, 'Get away from me, I don't need your help'. Not long after recovering, in the same match again, Charlie did Vince with a similar tackle. Vince couldn't talk as he attempted to tell Charlie what he would do with him once his feelings came back to his body.

Vince's work rate on both attack and defence was very high and he would always bolster our defence by continually shouting. I remember once against Halifax in a hard match at Thrum Hall. I tackled Jack 'Wilki' Wilkinson one on one, 'Well done Wilfy, up and back in line now,' called Vince. The next tackle I took big John Thorley one on one, 'Another good 'un Wilfy' shouted Vince. The third tackle on the trot I made, again one on one against a much bigger man, was on Albert Fearnley and Vince meant it when he shouted, 'Come on Wilfy, don't lay there all bloody day, get back in line', that was the strength of the man.

Vince was forever busy, like a modern day hooker, always in and around the ball. His presence against our opposition had an effect on their play too. Bob Dagnall, the international hooker, who, although being a St Helens lad, had signed for Rochdale Hornets and he told of the Rochdale coach who used to tell the Hornets team, every time they were playing Saints, that Vince was out injured, just to boost their confidence. What happened when they found out that he was playing is anybody's guess.

Vince had an unbelievable determination. Unbending, never diminishing, he was a one-off. Jim Sullivan used to tell Vince on the Tuesday, 'You're not playing this weekend. You need to rest those elbows'. Vince always had a problem with swollen elbows. Then on Thursday the coach had thought about it and said, 'I would like you to play Vince' and he would be at it again. Vince rated the hard, tough type of forward and he rated several who would stand their ground and still play football. He rated Brian McTigue of Wigan and Johnny Whiteley of Hull very highly and Derek 'Rocky'

Turner of Oldham, then at Wakefield Trinity, Dick Huddart and Stan Owen of Leigh similarly with the big hitter Charlie Winslade in there too. Vince used his aggression in the correct places too. We played the touring Australians and to get in their faces early, Vince stood opposite the big Aussie enforcer, Noel Kelly and looked straight at him, inches from his face. 'Is your name Ned Kelly?' Vince asked 'Because if it is, the outlaw must have been your dad. Well we shot him and I'm going to eat you today!' Kelly looked dumbfounded. That was pure, rough, psychology and was done so Kelly would be looking for Vince and not us young kids as we were then.

Vince was aggressive but rarely the aggressor, except for a game at Featherstone Rovers once when we had been beaten in the Challenge Cup and returned to Post Office Road in the league match. Right at the end of the game there was a flare up between around ten players, fighting all over the field. Glyn Moses was at it with the Featherstone stand-off, Joe Mullany and I was against a tough half-back, Alan Marchant. Vince was involved one on one with a Rovers forward when another Featherstone man came at Vince from the side with a 'cheap' shot. The referee ended the match and with it ended the fight too. Except that Vince was upset at the sly dig that the Featherstone man had given him and in the bath area of the dressing rooms, the bath being communal, a rumpus started involving this forward and Vince. The bath cleared very quickly as the two big men got at it and suddenly it was realised that Vince's opponent was under water, gurgling! Jim Sullivan jumped in, fully clothed and with some help bundled Vince into our dressing room. The 'cheap hitter' was found to be battered but OK and Vince settled down again.

In a match at Thrum Hall, our stand off 'Todder' Dickinson ventured too near the scrum when running with the ball and Jack Wilkinson kicked him up the backside. Out of the scrum dived Vince and caught big Jack off balance. Vince was on top when they were pulled apart and big jack was in a state, cut up a bit. But that was the man; nobody took liberties with his teammates. He rarely started any fight but he finished a few.

In a game a Central Park, only a few weeks away from a Wembley final, Vince went down heavily in a tackle and his knee ballooned up. Spotting the injury the Wigan pack played on it and Vince was under pressure. Austin Rhodes and myself, the two smallest in the team, decided to help Vince as best we could and when big Frank Collier and the tough Brian McTigue were trying to rough Vince up, we would run in and try pulling these big men away from Vince. After the match, laid in that big bath at Wigan, Vince said, 'Where are those two little lads who helped me out? Wilf and Austin, my little sparrowhawks!'

After Vince went to Widnes and we played against him, he would knock us down in a fair tackle, without it being extra tough and whisper, 'Get up you little monkey, I've not hurt you'. One little thing I remember about him was as young single men we would have a Saturday night out, sometimes six or seven players and all would shack up at any of the team's houses, like youngsters do. When it came to breakfast time and one of the mums was beginning to prepare ten breakfasts, Vince always was the one who helped make the meal. And sing. Last hour Saturday nights you couldn't get him off the stage. He used to ruin a lot of good songs but if his brother Dennis was with us the pair would sing a duet, 'Scarlet Ribbons' and to be honest that wasn't too bad.

A very great man. Great men are always someone's idol and Vince was mine. In the dressing room Austin and I would be sat either side of him, just to be near him. And the best thing is that he still is a very good friend. He is a gentleman and a hero. ***Wilf Smith***

Alex Murphy (St Helens, Leigh, Warrington, Lancashire, England, Great Britain)

I walked into the Saints dressing room full of confidence and cockiness after I had just signed with them. I had watched Vince since I was a kid and rated him above all others. I didn't know him personally though so when he started to tell me how to play scrum-half and when to run round the 'blind' side of the scrum, I was offended. 'How long have you played at scrum-half then, I thought you were a loose forward', I cheekily said, after all I played in one of God's chosen positions, a scrum-half, I wasn't going to let a forward talk down to me, especially when I was sixteen years old! Vince, the master, quietly explained that I had better listen to him as one of his many jobs on the field was to look after me and stop those other big, bad loose forwards hurting me or slapping my backside and sending me to bed. I listened, I had to. The man was THE man.

He took some getting to know, then, like a bolt of lightning, it struck home. He was a senior professional in our whole game, not just at Saints and you had to win his respect. Vince never said he would do what he couldn't do, although there were not many things that he couldn't do. This man could do most things with consummate ease. Whatever he asked you to do worked. As long as you gave whatever it was you were doing 100%, win or loose, it was OK with him.

Giving 90% was no good whatsoever. I sometimes believed when I first met him that he was my guardian angel. He took care of me so much on the field of play it was like having a personal minder and when we went to places like the Watersheddings in those days with the likes of Derek Turner, Sid Little, Ken Jackson and Charlie Winslade in their pack, looking after a cocky little sod like me was a job and a half.

His fitness was and still is in St Helens, legendary. He would run the 14 miles to training from his home in Widnes to the ground at Saints and sometimes run it BACK as well. He was a special breed of man – thinking about it anyone who jumps off the Runcorn Bridge must be special, or crackers, and he most certainly was not crackers.

Respect was the big thing in Vince's life. You earned his and he earned yours. He would not just take or give respect, he insisted that the special commodity should be earned. How could you win his respect? It was fairly easy, just prove yourself a man! Stand your corner in all things in life and he was your friend but never forget that if you had his respect then he wanted yours. He insisted that you learn your trade as a forward or a back and play as consistently well as you could and always listen to older players, they can teach you things.

Whatever Vince Karalius got out of life, in football or business, he earned. Nobody gave him anything. He saw what he wanted and went for it with everything he had. The strangest thing about Vince, and this is perfectly true, was that during a game he was the greatest professional I ever played with or against. He would do whatever was required to win, within the laws of the game, and was iron-hard against opponents, brutally hard some times, but after the game, when the emotions had softened, he was the nicest and most gentle man I have ever met. He could go through every emotion there was during a game and he could be very emotional on occasions afterwards. He had no sense of fear whatsoever and was the most consistent perfectionist I have ever known. If he made an error in a game he would work on what ever was needed so as never to make that mistake again.

The worst thing you could say to Vince was, 'You can't do that', if you did say it, then he would go and do it. He was one of the leading lights on the successful 1958 tour of Australia and New Zealand. He had a memorable tour. In the game in which Vince is supposed to have kicked Peter Dimond, I was there, I saw it all. For weeks the Aussie newspapers had said what this big, strong Peter Dimond would do with Mick Sullivan and Vince, when they came in with their crash tackles. Anyway, there had been clashes throughout this game between us and New South Wales in Sydney, most players having a go at some time or other. Dimond gets clear down the wing and Vince is the final tackler between Dimond and a try. A big man who could run, Dimond set his stall out to shift Vince good and proper but on impact of the tackle Vince picked him up like a baby and placed him over the touchline, out of play, a cracking tackle and one of Vince's specialities. Big Dimond bounces up, never having ever been flattened this way before and heads, at pace, straight at Vince who simply pushed that huge fist of his right on Dimond's chin. Down he went again but didn't bounce up this time. The referee, Mr Col Pearce, sent Vince off and his report said that Vince had kicked Dimond. This was a lie, punched him in self defence, yes, kick him, no way. But it was the reaction from the crowd that was strange. The 52,963 people booed and jeered as Vince took the long lonely walk across the Sydney Cricket ground towards the old dressing rooms and small gateway that Don Bradman had passed through so many times. The hissing and catcalls followed Vince right to the little gateway, then, Vince did something very strange himself. He stopped dead at the gateway and turned around to look at the 'hill', the notorious grass bank where the spectators picnicked at cricket tests and where the red necked, tough Aussie 'hard men' stood at rugby league tests, and all around the Cricket Ground it fell silent, everywhere as if to pay tribute to this 'wild bull'. That is true, it went quiet, it was eerie! The Aussies will give us nothing so to call Vince 'the wild bull of the pampas' was an honour indeed.

Another true and straight story happened in the famous Second Rorke's Drift Test in Brisbane. We had to win this test to keep the series alive as we had lost the First Test in Sydney. In no time at all we had Alan Prescott our captain playing with a badly broken arm and Wigan's Dave Bolton off to hospital with a broken collar bone. Vince was limping along with Eric Fraser at full-back and poor old Jim Challinor could hardly walk never mind run. We were up against it in good style. Tackling like never before and taking a hero's lead from Alan Prescott who stayed on the field and played and tackled with only the one good arm, we found ourselves in a winning position going into the last ten minutes. Vince had taken it upon himself to play at stand-off. He winked over at me and whispered, 'Work the run around Spud'. Now this was a little move we used at Saints but we had a full team then and Vince was wanting to work it with him at stand-off and normally he would have been at loose forward. 'Hang on Vinny, it won't work' I said. He gave me that steely glare, 'Run around' he growled. I gave him the ball and he offered a challenge for the Aussies to knock him over by him charging at their stand-off, sucking their loose forward and inside centre into him too as he stood up in a three-man tackle and slipped the sweetest pass to me – running around the back of him – that he had ever given. The pass sent me clear and I managed to cross for the perfect 'Saints' try and the Test was ours, the brave 11 and a half Great Britain men against the might of the Aussies.

Vince was magnificent throughout a long career and I consider myself fortunate to have played alongside this fine man for part of that career. I will just say that I hope one day to arrive in heaven. Vince will be there and I only hope we are in the same team. *Alex Murphy.*

George Parsons (St Helens, Salford, Wales)

Vince was a very confident and fit youngster when he first came to St Helens. He had a very tough attitude towards the game and always wanted to be a winner. He started his career as an outstanding A teamer and when Jim Sullivan came on the scene at Saints, Vince took to him and his style of coaching immediately. I remember him having a particularly strong game at Wembley in 1956 against Halifax, when he played with a torn ear. It was not that obvious that he would make it when he first came to Knowsley Road as he was not the biggest of players but he was very tough and determined and when he came out of his National Service he was much bigger and stronger than when he went in. Vince turned out to be an excellent forward and a fine worker for the St Helens club and obviously a key figure in international rugby.

He was a devil in the dressing room with his special way of preparing for games. Sometimes we would think he was not turning up but with seconds to spare he would breeze into the dressing room as if nothing was wrong. Jim Sullivan was good for him and Vince warmed to Jim's homespun philosophy. I used to smile when Jim would say, 'Whoever runs against so and so, don't bother side stepping or swerving, go straight through him as he can't tackle at all.' Vince ran like that every time, straight through them and it was amazing how many times he broke through. A fine forward was Vince. *George Parsons.*

Neil Fox (Wakefield Trinity, Bradford Northern, Hull KR, Huddersfield, Bramley, Yorkshire, England, Great Britain)

In the time of my career there were three outstanding loose forwards, Derek Turner, Johnny Whiteley and Vincent Karalius. Derek and Vince were of the same mould, tough, uncompromising, give nothing away, hard men who were also very skilful players. Johnny was of a different style, the athletic, fast moving ball player and a renowned good footballer. Derek and Vince played the tougher style, based on the rugged, stand up and knock 'em over type of play. To be honest Derek would get my vote as just the better of the two but there was little between them. Vince was a terrifically hard and skilful player and had a tremendous understanding with his half-back partner, Alex Murphy. As a tough tackler and gifted close-in ball handler Vince thrilled the Australian spectators on the 1958 tour and how on earth he missed the 1962 tour is one of the mysteries of our game.

Vince, like most hard men on the field, was an absolute gentleman off it. He was tough and would take no prisoners during a game but again he was not a dirty player. Hard, yes, he played to the extent of the laws of the game but never ventured into the dirty tactics beyond the laws and he was a straight shooter, a very honest man. Vince was a talent that only comes along very rarely and how lucky we were to see the Karalius, Turner, Whiteley combination together in one era. I know that Derek Turner had great respect for Vince and if Derek Turner rated you then you were a good one. He would say, 'St Helens next week, that tough bugger Karalius will be waiting for us, but he's a good 'un' To gain as much respect as he did on that 1958 tour from the Aussie public speaks volumes for Vince's ability. He is a member of the Rugby League Hall of Fame and of the Hall of Fame at the St Helens club which again tells of his prowess. A truly great player and gentleman. **Neil Fox.**

Jim Mills (Halifax, Workington Town, North Sydney, Widnes, Wales, Great Britain)

One of the most honest men I have ever met. A great friend of mine whom I speak to regularly on the phone. A true professional who maintains his professionalism to this day. When he told you something it was spot on. One way of epitomising Vince's thinking was if you were right with him, he would be right with you. I left England to go play for Roy Francis at North Sydney, in Australia, and had to cry off the very successful 1970 tour of Australia and New Zealand that was coached by Johnny Whiteley and captained by Frank Myler, but came back home in 1972 and went down to my parents' home in Cardiff. Jim Davies was the Widnes chairman then and Vince drove down to Cardiff to see if I was interested in joining him at Naughton Park. I had offers on the table from Bradford Northern and Wigan but after listening to Vince and his plans I decided to join Vince as he had talked me into it. I knew that Vince was big in the game and that he was very well respected too. A great bloke who only asked that you be loyal and true to him and he would return that loyalty.

When I returned from Australia I weighed around 23 stones, Vince advised me to reduce and I used to go round to his home in Widnes and he would put me through a gruelling weights session, then we would go running across the fields around where Vince lived. He was still 100% fit and he made you feel that you too should be fit when you saw him in action. I was not able to get proper match fit and although I was losing a bit of weight I was still way off the levels Vince wanted. One day at the Widnes ground Vince took me to one side and laid it on the line to me, 'Jim, this is just no good to either you or me', he said, 'You're letting yourself down because of a lack of fitness'. So we ran again over the fields and I really got down to it and by the time the cup ties came around in 1975, we were all fit as fiddles and I was down to 17 stones.

Vince had this bloody big heavy punch bag hung in his gym as he used to help train a cracking young boxer, Tony Strong, from Widnes. 'I've got just the thing for you, Jim' he said and had me punching this bag doing two minutes punching with one minute rest, for what seemed like hundreds of rounds. My weight rolled off under Vince and he brought me back to a good playing weight and gave me back my playing appetite. Because of the great weight loss I was yards quicker whilst still a big lad.

With that extra pace, Vince coached me to run that bit wider out. It was great for me as I started enjoying my rugby again and it was all down to Vince's enthusiasm and his fitness know-how. The try I scored at Wembley against Warrington was down to my new-found fitness as I sprinted over after a 60 yard break, actually it was about a 20 yard run but it gets longer every time I tell the story! We had prepared the Karalius way with a few days running up and down the sands at Southport then to the club's hotel at St Albans and on to a Wembley win.

You know, Vince loved genuine hard lads. He would sit in the bath after training and talk about the game, many times until the water was clap cold, but we all sat there listening because he was genuinely interesting and so passionate about the game. I remember when in Australia being asked to appear on the Frank Hyde Show, a rugby league talk show. The other guest was Rex Mossop who had played at Leigh and also for New South Wales and the full international Aussie side. He was a big guy but admitted that he was scared to death of tangling with Vince, who had seen him off a couple of times in good style. Mossop said he had broken out in cold sweats and dreamed of Vince's face all night on the eve of playing against him. I rated and still rate Vince because he is a credit to life itself and is respected throughout the world of rugby league. A wonderful man. *Jim Mills.*